T0323496

Seeking the Perfect World

Consider this book your invitation to the most exciting party of the century. We have invited you and some of the greatest minds of our species to dance, share cake, and ponder the age-old question: how can we make our world better? *Seeking the Perfect World* guides readers through thoughtful discussions of twenty-first-century challenges while providing everything needed to critically engage with current events and personal dilemmas.

This book explores topics humans have discussed for centuries ... and more recent developments. We discuss what is human nature, why humans go to war, international relations, education, animal rights, transhumanism, artificial intelligence, and more! Chapters introduce readers to different philosophies (and philosophers) and prompt nuanced reasoning via Socratic questions and thought experiments. Not only will this book enable readers to understand the complexities of some of the most pressing global challenges, but it will also provide a grounding on philosophical, sociological, and economic thinking and ideas.

Whether you are dipping your toes into philosophy for the first time, or you are a bright, curious teen seeking interesting conversations on the current events and global challenges, or a parent seeking ways to discuss difficult topics with your child – this book will provide you with the language and strategies needed to understand your own views and feelings while engaging in civic discourse. Come chat with philosophers, challenge your critical thinking, and expand your understanding of our world: past, present, and future.

Karem Roitman, Ph.D. (DPhil Oxford) is a lecturer in political philosophy and global development for the Open University and a consultant and public speaker on education, creative leadership, diversity, and belonging. She is also Director of Thinkers Meet Up Ltd (TMU), which runs enrichment courses for gifted and 2e students. She has worked in education for over 20 years, teaching from primary to postgraduate students, and training hundreds of teachers around the world on project-based learning, and twenty-first-century skills. She is a passionate advocate for inclusive, intercultural education, and critical global citizenship.

Seeking the Perfect World

A Critical Discussion of Global
Challenges for the Bright and Curious

Karem Roitman, Ph.D.

Routledge
Taylor & Francis Group

NEW YORK AND LONDON

Designed cover image: © Getty Images

First published 2025
by Routledge
605 Third Avenue, New York, NY 10158

and by Routledge
4 Park Square, Milton Park, Abingdon, Oxon, OX14 4RN

Routledge is an imprint of the Taylor & Francis Group, an informa business

ISBN: 978-1-032-60189-2 (pbk)
ISBN: 978-1-032-62012-1 (ebk)

DOI: 10.4324/9781032620121

Typeset in Times New Roman
by Newgen Publishing UK

For Isaac and Juan David – may you have many parties with philosophy

Contents

Acknowledgements

This book is the result of many years discussing philosophy with brilliant thinkers of all ages, from all around the world. Teaching philosophy to younger people is such a joy, a great honour, and a huge challenge. Brilliant, honest, young people, with no preconceptions about philosophers, no cultural baggage telling them some ideas are 'great', will come at ideas with sharp, merciless, questions. And they will come at my teaching equally harshly. They will let me know if a story is boring! They will find loopholes! They will ask questions that push my knowledge. These young people have taught me to rethink everything I was taught, to become a better communicator, and to have fun even with the most serious philosophies. They have been my teachers, not of philosophy, but of teaching. There are so many of you I need to thank – for your conversations, your questions, your jokes ... and most of all for sharing your precious time with me. Thank you.

This book, and all that I have been able to learn, could never have happened without the work of my parents – so they should always be mentioned. Thank you for the books you brought home, which opened the world of thinking to me. Thank you for moving across the world to make education available to me. And thank you for challenging me to think through my views. In particular, thank you for believing I could be a writer.

Speaking of education – my gratitude to the two professors who made me fall in love with political philosophy, and the professor who challenged me to take justice to the world: Jack Crittenden, Terence Ball, and Jose Mendez. This book would have never happened if I had not learnt about justice and rights, and questioned my own ideas, under your guidance.

Over the last few years, I have had the delight and honour of working with a group of brilliant scholars at *Thinkers Meet Up*. They have inspired me deeply. They are passionate about their subjects, always curious, always ready to jump into adventures. They are amazing educators. And they are great friends. Jo, I am so glad we met all those years ago. You are endlessly brilliant, insightful, witty, and knowledgeable. Always ready for a quick intellectual chat. I am so grateful for the critical feedback you gave some of these chapters, for all the wisdom you have shared, and for your warm support and friendship. Stuart, thank you for all the good advice and fun chats, for being an amazing collaborator, and for sharing your knowledge so generously. You are so humble in your genius, so ethical in your teaching, so passionate about making a difference. Chrissie, you are pure gold. Your kindness, brilliance, support, and humour have kept me sane in insane times. This book would simply not be possible without your help. May your beautiful writing inspire many. Debbie, Caroline, Radhika, Caroline E-S, Wing, Nalin, Jen, Camille, Nour, Paul, Moira, Josephine, Laura, Wayne, I have learnt so much from all of you. Thank you.

I write at home. On my bed, mostly, or in the kitchen. Writing happens amid the lovely chaos of daily life. It is inspired by this noise and adventure. And my life is filled by the most wonderful and handsome men. Simon, Isaac, Hux (and Flash), thank you for listening (willingly and unwillingly) to me as I test out material on you ☺. Simon, thank you for sharing your brilliant mind, for your perseverance and hard work against all odds. You are heroic. Supporting a Latin Kat in adventures take a fearless Scottish Oso. Chaqui, thank you for giving me such mature, kind, and thoughtful feedback during conversations. Morrongo thank you for your editing and critical challenges. Gratitude. And Flash … Mimiaou says hi. Les amo.

Introducing the Party

A Time-traveling Affair to Do
Political Philosophy

1 Time Traveling to Party with Philosophers

I often like to imagine what I would do if I had a time-machine. If I could travel to anytime (and anywhere!), when and where would I go? Where would *you* go?

I think I would visit a revolution. One of the great upheavals that changed human history, brought down governments, sought a new world … Perhaps I would head to France in 1789 to hear discussions about justice, liberty, and equality. I would join the masses to experience the fervour and madness that made the fight for change so bloody … I have always wondered how people can become so violent, how a revolution about justice can become so unjust … but then I would like to take off before my head ended in the guillotine. Revolutions are never safe, whatever side you are supporting!

Or I might go further back and walk among the Incas. I wonder what it was like to live in the great Tahuantinsuyo.[1] What did Cuzco look like when it was in its glory? I might become one of the messengers who ran along the Andes carrying messages between the Inca, the emperor, and his officers. The chasqui, as they were called, were so fit that if the Inca asked for fish while in Cuzco, one of the highest cities in the world, the chasquis would be able to relay the message to the coast and bring back fresh fish in less than 48 hours – even though the coast was over 200 miles from Cuzco. Yet again, I am not a great runner, so my career as a chasqui might end up badly. Time travel seems easier than running up and down the Andes.

Maybe it would be better to go into the future and see what human life is like a thousand years from now. Will we manage to learn from our errors and avoid environmental disaster? Have we traveled to another planet? Are all our brains wired to a global internet of some sort? Are there still countries?

I have so many questions about the past and the future! Some of my questions are silly. I wonder, for example, who thought it was a good idea to roast coffee beans that a cat had eaten and pooped? Did they find the poo and wonder 'hey, it looks like a coffee bean in there, let's cook this poop-coffee and see if its tasty'. Seriously, cat-pooped coffee?![2] Was it a dare? Why?

DOI: 10.4324/9781032620121-2

However, some of my questions are serious. Questions that humans have been asking for centuries. Why are we so unable to get along? Why has there been so much violence and death in our history? Why are we still killing each other now?! Why is there so much poverty? How can creatures who can pen poetry and ponder the nature of quantum particles, also create terrible weapons and let people starve?

I guess there is one big question that drives my curiosity. How can we make our world better? How can we make utopia?

Utopia is an ideal world. A perfect world.

What would an ideal world look like? Everyone wearing silky togas with flowers in their hair, eating vegan cakes? Or everyone living in their own little cave with robots to do all the chores? A world where everyone is free to do whatever they want ... or a world where everyone follows rules to make sure everyone is safe? Which is an ideal world, which is a nightmare?

What if I could use the time machine to bring together some of the greatest minds that ever lived and discuss these questions with them? Imagine having a meeting, a party, where all the greatest minds of our species could come together and discuss what we need to do to make our world better – to try and reach utopia.

Of course, this gets tricky. Who should be invited? Some estimate that 100 billion humans have existed. There are surely many brilliant people we know nothing about, perhaps because they lived before history was written. Or perhaps because what they said, what they thought, was never written down, or was burnt or stolen, or simply did not survive into our time. Perhaps because they were women, or of a different religion, or people who were enslaved, their ideas were not considered worth saving and are now lost to time.

If I put you in charge of the guest list, whom would you invite?

Do we invite leaders of ancient kingdoms? Great scientists? Brave warriors? Could we learn anything from dictators and thieves? Do only those who do good have good to teach? Can we learn what not to do from past evil? Not sure how I would feel about attending a party filled with a bunch of tyrants ...

Clearly, we have to limit the number of guests, otherwise we will just have chaos. Let's not even consider the issue of multiple languages, and the fact that languages evolve with time. We will assume that all our guests understand each other – like in Star Wars, where in a galaxy far, far away, somehow most creatures seem to have at least a rudimentary understanding of English ... so let's imagine we all somehow speak Esperanto[3] and can understand each other. And taking inspiration from Star Wars, let's open the invitation also to fictional creatures, if you wish.
So, whom would you have join us?

Given our limited time, I suggest we focus on those who have spent most of their time thinking about the best way to live. Those who have sought wisdom and thought about what we should think about, how we should think, why we should think. That is, I think we should invite philosophers. And Yoda. Because he is green and small and wise. Even if not real.

Let's open the door to the house and see who comes into our imaginary 'Philosophers' Party'. In the text below I am going to transcribe just a few snippets of this imaginary evening of time travel, interesting discussions, and, why not, some funky dancing.[4]

As you read this, you might feel overwhelmed by lots of new ideas and names. Don't worry. You will encounter many of these philosophers again in future chapters and you will have an opportunity to learn more about them and what they argued. For the moment, just listen along, and see what you think of the different ideas presented.

The Philosophers' Party

Socrates comes in first. Socrates is barefoot because he hated wearing shoes. Can't blame the guy, there is nothing more relaxing than taking off your shoes when you are home … but not so sure about walking around the whole city barefoot and then walking into my house … should I ask Socrates to wash his feet? I decide to just not think about it. We can give special allowances to the father of western philosophy.

As soon as he comes in, Socrates starts asking questions. Why are we here? Why did I think it was a good idea to bring people together for a discussion? Why did I choose him and not someone else from his time? How did I decide he was wise … woah! Slow down there, Socrates! We know asking questions is sort of what you do to get people thinking but let's slow down a little.[5] I offer Socrates some sparkling water. The bubbles amuse him enough to give me some time to let other philosophers in.

Socrates reminds us of what philosophy is all about: curiosity, seeking knowledge, seeking understanding, seeking truth. *Philosophy* means the *love of wisdom.*[6] And we can only find wisdom by asking questions, by being curious. Wisdom comes from questioning our ideas, our experiences, from reflecting on what we think and what we do.

Think about what reflection is. A reflection is light bouncing off something – say a banana! If you use different mirrors – concave/convex – different lenses – magnifying lenses, coloured lenses – light will reflect differently, and you will see different aspects of this banana – some real, some distorted. When we are considering an idea or an event, questions are like lenses/mirrors. They help us see the event from different perspectives, in different ways. Questions help us understand why something happened, why something is believed, and what might be the consequences of this idea or event.

If we don't ask questions, we might assume the first way we see something is the only way to see it – even if what we are seeing is a distorted reflection through a funny mirror! Or we might simply believe what others tell us is right.

The more we ask, the more we realise what we don't know. The more we ask, the more we might start to understand that we have assumed some ideas as true for no reason, or for faulty reasons. Questions force us to re-think what we believe, the way we live, how we act.

Other philosophers are now appearing in the house. Some look rather dazed and confused – being whipped through spacetime will do that to you. Is that … yes, that is Frederick Nietzche arriving in an Übertaxi![7] Other philosophers simply 'pop' into the room. Hegel checks his watch as he comes in – right zeitgeist? Some philosophers are also perplexed at what they find in a modern western house. Yoda is moving things around with 'the force' just for giggles … Once everyone is seated, I thank everyone for coming. 'The purpose of our meeting', I explain with grand gestures, 'is to discuss what we need to do to reach the perfect world'.

'You mean, the world of the forms?', questions Plato. He sits with elegant ease next to Socrates, his teacher. The Platonic forms are the perfect ideals of each thing. The Platonic form of a cat, for example, would be the ideal form of a cat, what all cats in our world are but pale shadows of.

I am just beginning to think about what the world of the Platonic forms might be when someone speaks up from the other side of the room. 'What we need is to stop doing what society tells us to do, and instead do what is right!', proclaims Nietzsche as he strokes his phenomenal moustache. He is referring to his idea of the Übermensch – the 'superman', – a person who chooses their own path, doing what is truly right, rather than what traditions and cultural values say is right.

'But if every man did whatever he wanted, we would have chaos. I could just, say, grab this stick and hit you! And take your food and … and take control! You would live in fear, that is, if you lived very long at all!' Thomas Hobbes is shaking with fear as he states this.

'Très triste', murmurs Rousseau trying to soothe Hobbes in French. 'Surely', Rousseau continues, 'It is not man who is savage and kills his brothers. Without rules we would not have this chaos you fear, Hobbes. Rather, it is society that corrupts man. It ties men with chains of greed, of competition, of evil. *Man is born free, yet everywhere he is in chains.*[8] A better world is a world away from this so-called civilisation'.

Carol Pateman shakes her head. 'I realise you gentlemen were born in a different era, so it might not be clear to you, but your discussion, your focus, misses women completely. It misses half of humanity! Certainly, the world will not get to a better place if we don't rethink our rules, our way of working, to include women.'

'Of course, it is not just women who have been ignored' a dark-skinned man speaks up. 'Non-whites have been treated as less than human. As less able to think, to feel. A better world can only be a world where each human is able to love themselves for who they are. A world where we don't wish we were born in a different skin. But perhaps this requires a revolution?' This is Frantz Fanon speaking. Fanon suffered from discrimination himself as a black man in Martinique, a French colony, and saw first-hand the impact of colonialism and discrimination among those he treated as a psychiatrist in Algeria.

I notice Immanuel Kant looking uncomfortable at this point. Kant lived in the eighteenth century and is perhaps most famous for his idea of the categorical imperative – he argued that we should try to live by rules that can be universally applied. For example, he argued that you should never lie. Never. Ever. Nope, not even then. If we agree that lying is bad, then we should never lie. There are no exceptions.

The categorical imperative also means you should never treat a person as a tool. A person is never a means to achieve something. Each person is an end in themselves. This again, is universal, no person should be used by another. But Kant also once wrote that people of different skin colours were of different intelligence, which supported the use of some people as slaves. Clearly, he is currently rethinking his assumptions.

This reminds me that our guests come from different times, from different cultures, from different ways of thinking. Some of what they thought was right, has been proven to be very wrong. Some of the guidance they gave has led humanity to terrible errors. Thinkers, philosophers, no matter how famous, are not always right. As you learn about their ideas it is important that you reflect and carefully judge what is correct and what is not. You can disagree with philosophers. Philosophers will certainly disagree with each other.

I overhear a disagreement on the other side of the room. Two female philosophers, Simone Weil and Simone de Beauvoir, are discussing what is needed for the perfect world. Simone Weil, perhaps in agreement with Fanon, wants a revolution to feed the poor in order to improve the world. Simone de Beauvoir shakes her head 'Surely, it is not about people eating, it is about people having a reason for existing. In a perfect world lives have meaning!'. Weil looks disgusted. 'Clearly', Weil replies, 'you have never been hungry!'.[9]

Should we be planning a revolution? The world is a hard place for so many. Millions go to bed hungry and cold every day. Millions more barely have enough. Is a revolution what we need to reach a perfect world?

At the mention of revolution, Edmund Burke jumps up nervously, 'No! it is too dangerous! Revolution is simply too dangerous. You open the floodgates and cannot know where the waters will lead. The very ones you want to help might end up dead, and society – all order, all knowledge – destroyed! Change must be slow, and conservative. Humanity has built what we have over centuries, it cannot be re-made in days!'

'But you cannot stop history', Marx's deep voice booms out. 'History is the history of class struggles. If you look at human history, this is what happens: those who do not have enough rise up and demand their fair share from those who have amassed wealth from the labour of the poor. In the perfect world this struggle will end, everyone will have what they need, and everyone will contribute what they are able to'.[10]

I suddenly see something shiny. Is that a cable coming out of a head? Is that … yes. That is Sophia, a robot designed in the late twentieth century, who talks and moves somewhat like a human. Talk about a technological revolution! Sophia was so impressive that the country of Saudi Arabia decided to grant it honorary citizenship. But I want to throw Sophia out! I don't think machines, robots, or AI, should be telling humans how to live a better life – why is she here? Did you invite her? Did another philosopher bring her in? Or, am I wrong? Should non-humans have a say in what an ideal world should be like? Should we ask AI for guidance into the future? After all, AI can analyse billions of pieces of data in seconds – more than any human ever could. It can find patterns, make informed predictions … should humanity turn to the machines it built to tell us how to live?

I quietly sneak up and turn Sophia off. Socrates is shocked as he was just about to ask it a question and I try to explain that Sophia is a machine and that I did not 'kill' it, since it was never alive. Philosophers from other centuries crowd around Sophia's lifeless body and Ada Lovelace and Alan Turing lead a discussion on whether powerful computers could lead humanity to a perfect world which takes a turn to discuss what being 'alive' means.

'It is not machines we should listen to. If we want a path to utopia, it is to Pachamama,[11] to all the life forms in it, that we must listen'. This statement comes from a striking woman with feathers in her hair and brown eyes that shine out from behind ceremonial red eye paint. She is Nemonte Nenquimo, an indigenous thinker from the Waorani community in Ecuador. 'You have all discussed only what humans need, what humans have done, what humans want. This is unwise. Humans cannot exist without nature. We are part of nature. An ideal world – this is the world Pachamama has already given us. We have abused it by letting greed lead us. The road to restoration is the road that listens to others, not just to humans'.

For many philosophers Nenquimo's words are strange. For a large part of western history humans have been thought of as different, separate, beyond and above nature. Nature has been understood as something we are meant to use, even to exploit and conquer, for our advancement. Thinking of ourselves as part of nature, as something like a tree, like a cat, a donkey … is just unthinkable.

A seventeenth-century philosopher speaks up – John Locke. 'All men should be able to freely choose how to reach a perfect world and …'

Without thinking I interrupt at the same time as Mary Wollstonecraft, a feminist philosopher, 'and women!' we both exclaim.

Diogenis, a Stoic philosopher looks up from his conversation with Kwasi Wiredu. 'When we say men, *and* woman' he says, nodding toward Wollstonecraft, 'surely we should consider people from all lands, coming together as equals, as we are all citizens of the world.' 'Yes', Wiredu, agrees, 'we must move away from divisions by nation, by country'.

Peter Singer speaks up, 'It is, indeed, our responsibility to help our fellow humans, whether they are next door to us, or in the opposite side of the world ...' 'Surely, you don't mean a world government?' interrupt a couple of philosophers at once. Suddenly a great commotion starts – between those who think the world could come together and those who think some type of division by country is still needed.

This is getting chaotic. Who knew philosophers were so feisty? Someone screams that 'No government is necessary!', that each person should decide on their own what to do, 'Anarchy!' Someone throws food across the room! More loud proclamations! I hear Hannah Arendt disagree loudly 'I was once a refugee! I *know* what happens when no state protects you, you have no rights!'

Then I notice a couple just sitting on the floor, peaceful amid the chaos. Marcus Aurelius, once the emperor of Rome and a Stoic philosopher is calmly meditating with Yoda. 'We cannot control how the stars move. There is so much out of our control. It is only our emotions we can control. Is the perfect world out of our control?' Aurelius asks.

Yoda giggles. There are still philosophers screaming. Burke and Marx seem about to hit each other with their walking sticks. Socrates is poking Sophia in the eye to try to see how it works.

Suddenly Yoda uses the force to lift up all the drinks in the room and ... everyone is wet.

Perhaps bringing philosophers from many ages and cultures together to discuss how to reach a perfect world was not the best idea. No doubt there are many great ideas being discussed in this party, but so many of the ideas contradict and overlap. And there is so much to discuss: should there be a world government, should we use AI for guidance, how can we 'listen' to nature, should humans try to live forever ...

Let's take a step back. Let's look at a few of these questions in more depth. This is what we will do in this book. We will look at some of the big challenges facing humanity. We will explore what can be done to make our world better in respect to each of these challenges. And we will explore different philosophers' ideas for inspiration as we discuss these challenges.

This book will not give you answers, it will ask you questions and give you ideas to consider. In a way, I guess, this book is trying to be Socrates in your life. Asking you to think, to question, and to think again. To seek wisdom.

If we all ask these hard questions and think hard, there is a chance we might just find a way to move our world to a better place in the future. This is the hope of this book.

There is a lot we will not be able to cover. And as the world evolves there will be new problems to address. Questions I have not thought about yet. Problems and possibilities that no human has even imagined yet. That will be your task. To solve the problems of the future, to explore new possibilities.

Bibliography

Arendt, Hannah. *The Origins of Totalitarianism.* New York: Harcourt, Brace & World, 1966. Originally published 1951.

Aurelius, Marcus. *Meditations.* Translated by Gregory Hays. New York: Modern Library, 2002. Originally written c. 170–180 CE.

Burke, Edmund. *Reflections on the Revolution in France.* Edited by J. G. A. Pocock. Indianapolis: Hackett Publishing Company, 1987.

Dietz, Mary G. "Simone Weil: The Way of Justice as Compassion." *The American Political Science Review* 93, no. 3 (September 1999): 697–698.

Fanon, Frantz. *Black Skin, White Masks.* Translated by Charles Lam Markmann. London: Pluto Press, 1986. Originally published 1952.

Hobbes, Thomas. *Leviathan.* Edited by Michael Oakeshott. New York: Simon & Schuster, 1997. Originally published 1651.

Huffman, Carl. "Pythagoras." In *The Stanford Encyclopedia of Philosophy* (Spring 2024 Edition), edited by Edward N. Zalta & Uri Nodelman. www.plato.stanford.edu/archives/spr2024/entries/pythagoras/.

Jean-Jacques Rousseau. *The Social Contract & Discourses.* Translated by G. D. H. Cole. London: Arcturus Publishing, 2017. Ebook. Originally published 1762.

Locke, John. *Two Treatises of Government.* Edited by Peter Laslett. Cambridge, MA: Cambridge University Press, 1988. Originally published 1689.

Marx, Karl. *Critique of the Gotha Programme.* Moscow: Progress Publishers, 1970. Originally written 1875.

Nenquimo, Nemonte. "'I Want People to Wake Up': Nemonte Nenquimo on Growing Up in the Rainforest and Her Fight to Save It." *The Guardian*, May 25, 2024. www.theguardian.com/books/article/2024/may/25/i-want-people-to-wake-up-nemonte-nenquimo-on-growing-up-in-the-rainforest-and-her-fight-to-save-it. (Accessed June 20, 2024).

Nietzsche, Friedrich. *Thus Spoke Zarathustra.* United Kingdom: Penguin Books Limited, 1974.

Pateman, Carole. *The Sexual Contract.* Stanford: Stanford University Press, 1988.

Plato. *The Republic.* United Kingdom: Clarendon Press, 1888.

Russell, B. *History of Western Philosophy.* 1st ed. London: Routledge, 1996. https://doi.org/10.4324/9780203487976.

Singer, Peter. "Famine, Affluence, and Morality." *Philosophy & Public Affairs* 1, no. 3 (1972): 229–243.

Wiredu, Kwasi. *Cultural Universals and Particulars: An African Perspective.* Bloomington: Indiana University Press, 1996.

Wollstonecraft, Mary. *A Vindication of the Rights of Woman.* London: Penguin, 2004.

2 What Is Political Philosophy? (Or Why You Should Read This Book)

Since you have picked up this book, I am going to make some assumptions about you:

- You are curious.
- You are bright (this tends to go together with curiosity!)
- You are interested in how our world works.
- You have opinions and questions about how our world *should* work.

You, my friend, are a perfect candidate to study political philosophy.

Political philosophy is the study of how our societies have been set up, and a discussion about how they *should* be set up and why. It looks at political ideas, political structures (like government), and political practices (like voting).[1] Something is political if it affects how power and resources are distributed. Political philosophy looks at big questions that affect the distribution of resources and power such as: are all humans equal? What is human nature? Who should be in charge (if anyone)? Should we try to make everyone happy? Who decides what is a want and what is a need?

Note that political philosophy is not like the natural sciences, it does not simply try to understand what exists. We are also trying to decide what we *should* do. That is, we take normative positions, we made recommendations. But these opinions need to be supported by strong, logical arguments. Philosophy doesn't just declare that a world-wide government is evil or wonderful. Philosophy debates *why* a global government might be good or bad, it looks at evidence, it seeks to be logical, it addresses counterarguments, it considers different perspectives.

Asking Questions

To understand a society, political philosophy needs to understand the people that make it up. Therefore, political philosophy often starts by asking questions

DOI: 10.4324/9781032620121-3

about the individuals that make up society – what are we as humans like? Are we naturally violent? Can we change our nature through education? Are we different from other animals? Are we god-like in some way?

Political philosophy deals with questions that have no easy answers. Questions over which wars have been fought – such as should humans vow down to God x or Goddess y? These are questions for which many are still willing to lay down their lives and, more troubling, questions over which some are willing to kill. Studying political philosophy, therefore, can be very emotionally charged. One of the goals of this book is to help you practice engaging with difficult debates not just emotionally but also rationally. This is a desperate need for our world. If we cannot debate hard questions without fighting, we have no hope of building friendships and communities with those we disagree with. And that is a terrible outcome: endless conflict and death.

Political philosophy also deals with questions that different cultures might answer differently. For some societies, for example, eating animals is just part of life. For other societies, certain animals are sacred and should never be hurt. For others no animals should be hurt in any way. And, of course, cultures change. At one point putting holes through parts of the body is seen as grotesque … then a few decades, or centuries, later, everyone is wearing multiple earrings. Cultures are porous: they are affected by those around them, those who come in, those who leave. Cultures are not static, new ideas, new 'revelations' emerge, things change.

This brings up a very difficult question: is there one true, right, answer for the questions political philosophy asks? If we search hard enough, look closely enough, use our minds … will we find the *one* right answer?

This, like many other questions in this book, is something I will not answer for you. But I will prompt you with further questions. For example, if there is no one right answer, if there are several possible answers, and they contradict each other (if one view is that we should all eat meat and another is that no one should eat any meat), how can we reach a compromise? Can we create stable societies with internal disagreements? Or can societies only survive if we are all the same?

Political philosophy asks you to reflect on your answers to big questions about how we should live. If you think a monarch should rule your country, for example, why do you think that? Are your views based on a careful assessment of what a monarch does for a country, or are they based on your traditions? On what your parents once told you? On what you read in a poster or saw on TV?

Political philosophy asks you to think critically. To avoid simply repeating what you have heard, or what you have assumed. To go back and investigate why you think as you do and to consider what are the implications or effects of your views.

For example, if you think that everybody should be given food by the government so no one is hungry, you need to think about: will everyone get the same food? What about people's allergies or religious preferences? Where will this food come from? Will farmers donate food? Will farmers be paid for the food? If everyone gets food, will this put people who sell food out of business? Will it make those who transport food wealthy? Will this make the rich even richer since now they no longer have to spend on food and they can spend that money on luxuries or on starting other businesses? Is this fair? It is ever right to let people starve? Now, if you think only some people should be given food by the government – how will you decide who? Will you feed only children – and let parents go hungry? Would you give more food to kids who do more exercise? Or, if you think no one should get food, would you be ok watching people starve to death?

Assumptions

Every action has consequences. Every thought has assumptions. As you study political philosophy you will explore these and become a better, sharper thinker.

'Assumptions?!', perhaps you are thinking right now, 'I don't assume things. I know!'

The thing about humans is that we all assume things. It is the only way to survive. For instance, if you go hiking and you come across some berries, unless you know otherwise or an expert tells you, you will assume they are poisonous. And you should! Please assume that all berries and mushrooms you find on your hike are poisonous unless you are 100% certain otherwise. Assume snakes will bite you if you pet them. Assume bears will eat you if you try to hug them. This will increase your chance of not dying in the woods! And like these assumptions we make many others. Assumptions are part of how humans make sense of their reality and find ways to stay safe.

We pick up assumptions from our surroundings and culture. If you grew up in a country that uses fish sauce for example, when you smell that strong smell, you assume food is being prepared. If you did not grow up in such a country, when you smell fish sauce you might assume something is terribly wrong in the kitchen.

The study of political philosophy requires us to become aware of our assumptions and the assumptions of our society. You might have grown up assuming that women are not good leaders. Or that animals are less important than humans. Or that rich people are evil, or wise. Or that your neighbours are your enemies. In this book we will explore a variety of social topics and try to figure out what assumptions we might have about these topics.

Different Perspectives

To look at something critically means to look at it with curiosity, asking questions to understand it in new ways, while seeking to uncover assumptions we might have about it. To think critically, it can help to try to use different perspectives. A couple of my favourite examples of exploring topics critically via different perspectives come from public bathrooms.

When you go to public toilets you might have come across automatic hand driers. I never gave these much thought until one of my sons categorically REFUSED to enter any bathroom that had these. He would run out screaming pants down, if need be, rather than be in a room with one of these driers. Why? I mean sure, they are a bit noisy, but come on. Just don't use one and move on, right?

I was not looking at this issue critically. I assumed they were just a bit loud. However, it turns out that if you are a toddler, given your height and the size of your ear canals, the noise these machines make hits your eardrums much harder. Hard enough to create damage. So, my son was simply protecting his ears from pain and possibly from permanent damage. I only realised this when Nora Keegan, then 9, published her research on hand driers (Keegan 2020). Nora thought about the issue critically, thinking about hand driers from a different perspective: from the perspective of smaller people.

Now a second – also toilet related – example. I remember once traveling to a country with squatting toilets (Turkey) with a group from the USA. My USA companions were aghast – to squat? How dirty! They would walk for blocks to find 'proper', 'clean' toilets. But if you think about it, squatting public toilets are more hygienic … you are not sharing a seat with many other naked bums. However, my friends' cultural assumptions preventing them from being critical thinkers (and possibly from keeping their bums clean). They assumed the toilets they had always used were cleaner than the toilets used in other countries. They did not stop to ask why they thought as they did. Was it based on evidence, or on what they were used to?

Critical and Creative Thinking and Philosophy

When we start thinking critically, we also start thinking creatively. When we ask questions, we start to think about how something could be different, in what other ways something could happen. We start to imagine. In fact, political philosophers are some of the most creative people out there. They spend years imagining new ways to organise society, new ways to understand our problems, new solutions for injustices, new ways to think about even what it means to be human.

As you read about the topics this book covers you are invited to be creative yourself. You might come up with different ways to understand and solve a problem. Fantastic. Be creative. Be brave. But remember to be critical. Don't assume things without proof. Don't be convinced by the views of others, no matter how elegant or cool, without seeing their logic and evidence.

You might wonder how political philosophy is linked to the rest of philosophy. Political or moral philosophy is usually seen as one branch of philosophy. However, I would like to argue that this type of philosophy holds other branches of philosophy within it. When we study how to live, how to create our world, we are asking questions about what we know about ourselves and our world (cosmology) and how we know this (epistemology); whether what we know is logical (logic); we are considering what is beautiful and how to create it (aesthetics); we are thinking about the right way to live (ethics); we might ask if there is a god/gods and how they think we should live (metaphysics).

This book will use political philosophy to explore some of the great issues that face humanity. Some of these issues have been around from the start of humanity (war, power, leadership), some of these issues are quite new, emerging only as our knowledge has progressed (artificial intelligence and cloning, for example*). The goal of this book is not to tell you what to think about any of these topics*. That is up to you. The goal of this book is to introduce you to topics you might not have considered before and to help you re-think issues that you might find familiar. My goal is to help you think critically and creatively. Ultimately my goal is to help you consider how to live. That is to help you become an ethical, critical, and creative thinker.

A Note on Feelings and Critical, Ethical, Thinking

Changing the way you think about something is not easy. If you have always thought, for example, that broccoli was poisonous and suddenly someone tells you it is food, you might feel confused! This is clearly a silly example, but there are lots of serious ones. For a long time, many humans believed Earth was at the centre of the universe and all other planets and the sun rotated around it. When scientists and philosophers stated that the Earth was just one more planet rotating around the Sun, people were confused. People were angry. Some people felt this offended god and the order he had mandated! Some people were sad and upset. Upset enough to want to hurt those who did not see the world as they did.

Finding out that your views are mistaken, trying to understand someone's completely different way of thinking, and changing your own views is not easy. It can be painful, embarrassing, even infuriating, to realise you have been mistaken. It can make you upset with those who taught you before or annoyed at those who are teaching you now.

Give yourself time to feel what you feel as you think new thoughts reading this book. Feelings are part of the process of learning and thinking. Note that as you discuss new ideas with friends and family they may also get upset. They might feel upset their own views are being questioned or that your points of view are no longer the same as theirs. Give them time to also think and feel their feelings. Come back together and discuss your points of view and remember that disagreeing with someone's ideas does not mean you cannot still like and love this person. We cannot let disagreements destroy our communities.

Through this process I think it is key to have good friends and trusted mentors you can depend on, to discuss, to ask questions. Someone able and willing to listen to your queries, ideas, and doubts and able to point out to you if you are making unwarranted assumptions or missing some information.

A Note on Philosophers Included and Excluded – Now and in the Past

Who should be our teachers?

This question, once you start thinking about it, is very important. In some societies only older people are seen as wise and able to teach. In some societies only certain men are listened to. In some, only those who have obtained educational degrees, or those who have hunted so many wild beasts, are held as wise and able to teach or guide.

But what if some of those wise teachers have also done terrible things? Should we still listen to them? This is a relevant question for this book. The philosophers discussed in this book came up with brilliant ideas and excellent tools to help us think. However, these philosophers were also ignorant in some areas and terribly mistaken in others. They might have discussed the need for freedom, for example, while also supporting slavery. They might have advocated for rules that could apply to all men, while refusing to consider women.

These philosophers were not fully critical, ethical thinkers in all areas of their lives. Some were led by their prejudices and biases. Some acted in terrible ways. Rousseau, for example, who wrote about children and education, who argued that children needed to be loved and cared for, abandoned his own children to an orphanage. Locke, who wrote about man's inalienable right to life, liberty, and property, invested in slave trading companies.

Should we not read or discuss philosophers who have participated in horrible acts or who have argued for terribly mistaken views? I think if we did this, we might soon find ourselves silently sitting alone. The reality is that most humans make mistakes. Most humans have held mistaken ideas at some point. But in the midst of their mistakes, they have also come up with some good ideas. I think we need to be very careful to never look up at people as though they are great. Idolising people – making them into heroes, idols, demi-gods – is always an error. Every person has great potential for both good and evil. Even the greatest thinkers can be terrible humans. We need to learn from good ideas, learn why bad ideas are bad, and do better than what was done in the past.

Think of philosophers as flawed, limited humans, who tried to think, had some good thoughts, and had many bad ones. You can do better than them in many ways. We expect you to do better. Learn from their mistakes. But the only way to learn from their mistakes is to critically explore their ideas.

One of the great errors of western philosophy is that it listened to only some voices. When Europeans landed on the Americas, for example, they burned the wisdom and knowledge of those who lived there already (the indigenous people). So much knowledge about the plants and animals of the land was lost. Different ways of thinking about humanity, nature, freedom, and power were erased. If indigenous people tried to speak up, they were ignored or killed. Of course, European colonisers thought what they were doing was right, that it was the best thing to do – because they were only listening to themselves. If they had listened to the voices of those they were meeting, of those who opposed colonisation and slavery, they might have realised the barbarity of their actions. They might have thought differently about how to build societies and how to explore the world.

If we are to seek wisdom, therefore, we need to listen to the voices we have ignored for centuries. When we want to think about the best way to live, the way to build a better world, we cannot only listen to 'dead white old men' – we need to listen to women, we need to listen to people from many countries, of different religions, of different cultures and points of views.

However, because of space, there are only so many voices represented in this book. And because I am trying to introduce some of the most well-known western philosophical ideas to you, the book will be weighted toward some of the more traditional philosophers. But please remember there are more voices, more knowledge to get. Look at the extra resources listed. Do your own research. Learn more than I know!

A Note on Judging Ideas

As you are reading and thinking about ideas, how can you decide what is and is not a good idea? One way to judge ideas is to consider their consequences. What impact will this idea have? Consequences, however, are not often immediately visible. When we think about the impact of an idea, we have to consider its immediate impact, what it may cause now, as well as its long-term impact, what impact the idea might cause 20, 100, even 1000 years from now. When humans came up with plastic, for example, we considered its usefulness – how it allowed us to keep things clean and packaged for a very long time without breaking like glass. But we did not consider that its long-life would result in plastic polluting every ecosystem in the world for centuries.

We might also consider the impact of ideas on different groups/beings/areas. Using animals to test drugs for safety, for example, is a great idea for humans who are kept safe from dangerous drugs. But it is obviously a terrible idea for the animals used in the testing.

We can also consider the logic of the idea. An idea can be dressed in elegant and convincing language. It can have the support of celebrities and great powers. But if it is built on poor arguments and bad logic, it is likely a poor idea. Slavery, for example, has been supported by quoting religious texts and practiced by powerful men and countries. But if we look at the logic of slavery: the idea that some people are inherently better than others and, therefore, have the right to own other human beings, abuse them and kill them, we realise that the logical basis for the idea is deeply flawed. There is no evidence to prove any group is better than others. And abusing and killing other humans is morally disgusting.

Starting the Book

I hope you have fun reading this book. This is not a novel you need to sit and read through to get to the end of the story. It is a collection of thinking bits. Take your time. Read a section and then chat about it with a friend. Or do some research. Or go for a walk. Move between chapters. Write your own chapter. Use this book as a tool to inspire deep thinking. And above all things, have fun.

References

Farr, J. "Locke, Natural Law, and New World Slavery." *Political Theory* 36, no. 4 (2008): 495–522. https://doi.org/10.1177/0090591708317899.

Ferrari, M., and F. Alhosseini. "Cultural Differences in Wisdom and Conceptions of Wisdom." In *The Cambridge Handbook of Wisdom*, edited by R. J. Sternberg and J. Glück, 409–428. Cambridge: Cambridge University Press, 2019.

Keegan, Nora Louise. "Children Who Say Hand Dryers 'Hurt My Ears' Are Correct: A Real-World Study Examining the Loudness of Automated Hand Dryers in Public Places." *Paediatrics & Child Health* 25, no. 4 (June 2020): 216–221. https://doi.org/10.1093/pch/pxz046.

Rousseau, Jean-Jacques. *The Confessions*. Baltimore: Penguin Classics, 1782/1995.

3   How to Read This Book

There are many ways to read this book. Of course, you can read this book from page 1 to 1000, left to right, as with other books written in Indo-European, Uralic, Turkic … languages. However, you do not have to do this. This book is written as a collection of essays, each of which looks at a specific topic. You can choose to jump around and read the topics you find most interesting. There is no order you must follow. For your ease, the essays have been combined into sections, loosely following the idea of a party with philosophers:

Introducing the party – A time-traveling affair to do political philosophy
1. Time traveling to party with philosophers
2. What is political philosophy? (or why you should read this book)
3. How to read this book
4. A quick note on utopias and dystopias

Excuse me, who are you? Starting the party with questions about identity and human nature
5. What do you want? Discussing the ideal life
6. Who makes you, you? Discussing identity
7. Why do we go to war? Discussing human nature and international relations

Who said you could dance on the table? Questions about rules, contracts, rights, and wrongs
8. Who should rule? Discussing the perfect government
9. How do you know that? Discussing the perfect education
10. Who owns what? Discussing ownership and reparations
11. Should humans be like geese? Discussing migration and citizenship

DOI: 10.4324/9781032620121-4

Should we eat a guest or 3-D print sushi? Questions about nature and technology
12. Should nature have rights? Discussing how humans relate to nature
13. Is having pets immoral? Discussing our favourite animals
14. Would you like to become a cyborg? Discussing transhumanism and Posthumanism
15. Should we be afraid of AI? Discussing the future of technology

Justice as a parting gift: Questions about language, beauty, and justice for the past and the future
16. How do you say knowledge? Questions of language, knowledge, and justice
17. Should the government pay for opera? Questions about art, beauty, and politics
18. Does the past affect the future? Questions about colonialism, knowledge, and justice
19. How can we build a just world? Questions about justice, diversity, and the future

Until we meet again
20. Conclusion

Each chapter in the book will invite you to consider imaginary scenarios, to think about a problem through multiple perspectives, creatively and deeply. Each chapter will consider different aspects of an issue – imagine it as a normal conversation you might have with a friend. The book is your friend. Feel free to answer the questions it asks, or to ask your own questions. Write your thoughts and feelings on the margins of the book (yes, this is a book to be written on! I think all books are!).

Write on the margins. Underline bits you find interesting. Ask questions. Write why you agree/disagree at the end of each chapter. Find articles that contradict what the book says and write me a letter to let me know what I missed. What I got wrong. Think about what you read and enter into a conversation with the book and with me. You don't have to agree with me or anything in the book. Ever. But you need to think about *why* you disagree. You need to be able to express your thoughts so that others can learn from you. And we all have to be humble enough to realise that we need to listen to each other. Because no one has all the answers or even all the questions. Socrates, when he was called a wise man, replied, 'All I know is that I know nothing'. Socrates' search for wisdom taught him humility, as there is always more to know. Learning can only happen if we are aware that others can see what we cannot. If you take nothing else from this book, take the idea that of the billions of humans who have lived, and the millions of philosophers who have sought wisdom, no one has gotten everything right. We can all do better by listening to each other kindly and humbly.

The last section of each chapter will present you with further questions to consider. Fun queries to ponder as you wait for the bus or brush your teeth! Deep questions you might continue to ponder for years.

There is so much to be said and thought about if we want to make our world better. This book is just the beginning. Use it to inspire your own research. Read it, discuss it with your friends, your neighbours, random people on the road. Respond to its ideas. Write me! The only way for us to move forward is by kindly discussing difficult questions. And if you get too upset about something, let Yoda throw some cooling water on you ☺

4   A Quick Note on Utopias and Dystopias

The word *utopia* was made up by Thomas More in the sixteenth century. More seems to have had a good sense of humour as he made up this word to mean two contradictory things at once – an oxymoron!

Utopia can be read as coming from EU-TOPIA – EU from the Greek for EUDOMONIA – which we might think of as flourishing or happiness, and TOPIA relating to place (think, for example, of topography).

So, utopia can be read as the place of flourishing or happiness.

However, utopia can also be read as coming from OU-TOPIA – which would be the place that does not exist.

So utopia is the perfect place of happiness, and also the place that does not exist. I imagine that More giggles every time someone uses this word. Was More trying to send us a message by creating this word? Was he saying that a place of perfect happiness and flourishing could never be?

Most people understand utopia to mean the perfect place. And in history there have been many, many attempts to build perfect places, perfect cities, perfect societies.

More's book *Utopia* described what its main character, Raphael, sees as the perfect society. In *Utopia* every house is the same and every ten years you get to move into a different house by lottery. This means there is complete equality and no private property. In More's *Utopia* few things have value. Gold and silver are seen as useless, so much so that they are used to make chamber pots. Everybody works and all public services in Utopia are free. There is religious toleration for all religions … but not for atheists. Those who commit crimes in Utopia or in other states can escape death by becoming slaves. And you would think twice about committing any crime or breaking any rules in Utopia, as disobedience is simply not tolerated. Does More's *Utopia* seem appealing to you?

While *Utopia* was just a book, you can visit an attempt at building a utopia in real life in Scotland. In the eighteenth century Robert Owens decided to set up New Lanark as an ideal society. New Lanark was built in response to the inhumanity and chaos Owen saw in the large cities of the industrial

DOI: 10.4324/9781032620121-5

revolution: families working long hours yet living close to misery; multiple people sharing a single dirty room as their home; dozens of families sharing a thoroughly disgusting communal bathroom; children ignored or forced to work in the same factories as their parents, often resulting in injuries or death.

Owen thought that these conditions made people angry, mean, and small-minded. If children could be brought up differently, he thought, they would grow up to be different. So, he set up New Lanark as a clean, welcoming, small village. Every family got their own two-bedroom house. Child labour was forbidden. Hitting children was forbidden. Instead of working, children went to school and were encouraged to be curious. Everyone had to work but everyone would be kept safe as well. You would be safe, but had to do as Owen instructed. You traded freedom for security.

Would you move to More's imaginary town? Or to Owen's factory town?

There are attempts to build utopias even this century. 'The Line' is an ambitious project by the government of Saudi Arabia to build a whole city in the shape of a line. From beginning to end The Line will be 106 miles but only 200 meters wide. A high-speed train will allow you to travel from one end to the other in less than 20 minutes. Once it is built, the city promises to hold up to 9 million people living vertically while being environmentally sustainable. As it is being built in a desert with very limited access to water, how this will work remains to be seen. The idea of building a large city from scratch, rather than to let a city evolve from the interests and ideas of its inhabitants, poses an interesting model. Can utopias be built without people, and then have people move in? Can city builders know in advance what people will want? What makes a perfect, or utopian, city?

Would you move to The Line?

While a few utopias have been proposed, attempted, and written about, many more dystopias have been created in fiction. Dystopias are, as the name implies, the opposite of utopias. Places where things are terrible. An interesting thing about dystopias in literature is that they often appear as utopias at first ... until you look more closely. In *The Giver*, for example, everyone seems happy, and society is flourishing ... as long as some things are not spoken about. This makes one wonder – does perfection always become corrupted and end in destruction? Or is seeking perfection a path to destruction?

In dystopian literature there is usually one value, one thing, that the society seeks above all other. This is the value they think is key for a utopia. In David Eggers' *The Circle*, it is transparency. In *The Hunger Games* it is peace. It might be a good value, such as justice, or happiness – as in *Brave New World*, or development, or peace. But to seek this value all else is sacrificed. To seek peace, the past is erased. To seek justice, violence is committed again and again. To seek happiness, experiences that can lead to unhappiness are forbidden. Suddenly human experience is limited, is controlled, is deeply imperfect.

We have to be careful when seeking change for our world. For each thing we gain, something might be lost. For everything we find, we might lose sight of other things. There is always a trade-off. Maybe in humanity perfection is, at least in some part, compromise. The imperfect is perfection?

References

Collins, Suzanne. *The Hunger Games*. New York: Scholastic Press, 2008.
Eggers, Dave. *The Circle*. New York: Alfred A. Knopf, 2013.
Lowry, Lois. *The Giver*. Boston: Houghton Mifflin, 1993.
More, Thomas. *Utopia*. 1516. Reprint, London: Penguin Classics, 2003.
Neom. *The Line*. www.neom.com/en-us/regions/theline. (Accessed June 10, 2024).

Excuse Me, Who Are You?

Starting the Party with Questions
About Identity and Human Nature

5 What Do You Want?

Discussing the Ideal Life

The philosophers gather around the snacks and nibbles we put out (is that … frogspawn? Ah! For Yoda …) We are discussing how one should live a good life. What does a good life mean?

German Philosopher Frederick Nietzsche (1844–1900) clears his throat after a mouthful of fruit. 'To consider how to live well', he starts, 'we should imagine we will live the same life over, and over, again, and again. Eternal recurrence. If tomorrow you woke up to relive today, and so on for eternity, would you be happy with your life?'

One might think of life as something that starts, happens, and ends. But not everyone thinks this way. For some life is eternal. And for some life repeats, a bit like a wheel or a spiral. You finish a cycle and then you start again. Indigenous American cultures and Buddhism, for example, see life as re-starting again and again.

If we had to live the same life without any changes over and over …, would you find such an idea wonderful or unpleasant? If you are living a good life, you might be happy to live this life again and again. If the idea of living the same life over and over makes you tremble, you are probably not living the best life. You need to think about what you would change to live a good life.

But what is a good life? Is it a life full of pleasure? Or full of sacrifice? One where you do whatever you want, or one where you consider how your actions affect others?

Congratulations!

You have won a once in a lifetime opportunity to live the life you have always wanted! To live *The Best Life Ever*!

This is truly a once in a lifetime opportunity because whatever you choose, you will have to live for the rest of your life! So, think carefully about your choice. You can choose one of the following options or you can make your own

DOI: 10.4324/9781032620121-7

proposal. But whatever you choose, once you turn the page … that is it. This is your life choice. For you and all those around you. So, choose carefully. Choose a good life!

A. You can live in a world with no rules! Here everyone can do as they wish, when they wish, how they wish. Total freedom. Want ice cream for dinner? Go for it! Want to set off fireworks on your roof at 2am? Go for it! Want to travel around the world making a living by showing off your ear wax sculptures? No one can stop you!

B. Never worry about safety again! In this option we promise you safety. Everyday there will be food. You will be warm and comfortable. You will have a safe house. We assure you no one can hurt you. No, you cannot choose what you want to eat – you might choose something unhealthy, against your long-term safety. Yes, you get far fewer choices, but you will be safe.

C. Who needs to experience the dangers of real life? In this life you can plug yourself into a state-of-the-art computer and live through a simulation. Your life will be imaginary, and created by machines that give you excitement, give you jokes, and let you rest. You will live the rest of your life on a comfortable chair plugged into the best computer simulation ever. Have fun, have adventures, even jump off a cliff and die without fear as nothing is real!

D. Make up your own option. But be fair – you must decide on clear rules.

What is your choice?

What is a good life has been endlessly debated. The problem is that you cannot have it all. If you want all freedom, for example, you must face danger. The freedom of owning a gun, for example, comes with the danger that someone else with a gun might shoot you. Or the freedom of accidentally shooting a person and having to live with guilt for the rest of your life. Similarly, the freedom to jump of a plane comes with the danger that the parachute might not open, and you will become a human tortilla.

But, surely, living with no freedom is also terrible.

Imagine having no fears, but also having no choices. Food is chosen for you to be healthy and safe. Your clothes are chosen to ensure you are kept at the optimal temperature and your body is safe from scratches or injuries. You are not allowed to do dangerous activities such as bungee jumping or skying. Any choice implies danger – because every choice implies a possible error. So complete safety means no choices. But you are safe.

Clearly both extremes are bad. Is there a compromise that would be ideal? How much freedom are you willing to give up for safety? Or, put the other way, how much safety will you sacrifice for freedom? Does it even make sense, however, to speak of partial freedom or partial safety?[1]

The challenge becomes greater when you realise that this is not just about you, but also about your family and all those you love. You might be quite happy with option A, to live a risky, adrenaline-filled life, with complete freedom … but will you want your grandmother to be in danger? Would you stand by when your five-year-old cousin decides to bungee jump from their window?

The nice thing about option C, you might note, is that it is not real. You can live all sorts of crazy lives – hurl yourself into a black hole and be spaghettified, try to be adopted by a pack of wolves, drive 200 miles per hour, eat dog food … without fear, because it is all a simulation. If you lose an arm, it is just a game, and you can get a new arm with the press of a button. But would you like to live just an imaginary life, rather than something more … real? Is an imaginary life, a life at all?

After all, what is safety or freedom if there are no risks? Perhaps safety and freedom only exist in opposition to each other – we feel safe, because we know we could be unsafe, we feel free because we are taking risks.

What Is Freedom Anyways?

Are we ever completely free? I might scream that I am 'free to fly!' for example, but unless I grow wings somehow, I am only free to jump around like a deluded penguin – sad little bird that cannot fly. My freedom to fly is limited by my lack of wings. To fly I require wings.

Freedom requires resources. For example, to be free to travel around the world I need money, a passport, and often visas. (Or I need wings and hollow bones – become a bird!) Or think about your freedom to eat. You might be free to eat but if you have no food … this freedom is kind of an empty freedom, no? Or if I am free to learn but have to spend all day working in a mine … am I really free to learn? We are talking here about what Isaiah Berlin termed *positive liberty – liberty to* achieve our goals and desires. Without resources – such as money, food, time – we cannot achieve these freedoms.

On the other hand, for my neighbour to be free to rest in peace, my freedom needs to be limited. Someone or something has to stop me from screaming and drumming at all hours (well, they say screaming, I say singing). My neighbour's freedom is what Berlin called *negative liberty*. It is a freedom *from* something. If you look around, you will realise that your freedoms are based on a variety of negative freedoms. You are free from people randomly entering your house because there are laws that punish such behaviour. You are free from being exposed to cigarette smoke because of laws that prohibit smoking in public places. It is interesting to think that some of our freedoms require less freedom for others.

Freedom is not simple. To be free to do different things we need resources – health, money,[2] support, books, food. To be free we need to limit the freedoms of others.

Is It All About You?

If freedom is doing whatever I want … what if I want to go and play the drums in my neighbour's garden in the middle of the night? Is that allowed? 'Definitely not!' yells my neighbour. My freedom to make noise, argues my neighbour, should stop where their freedom to be in peace (and sleep at night!) starts. My neighbour is using what philosopher John Stuart Mill called the *harm principle*. That is, an individual's freedom needs to stop where it starts to harm another person.

Of course, we could question what harm means. If I paint my house purple with yellow dots and my neighbours complain that I harm their eyes, should I limit my freedom to be creative to protect my neighbours' artistic sensibilities?[3] Does the type and severity of harm make a difference when we decide what freedoms need to be restricted for the sake of others? Is harm the same if I harm your car, your pet, or you? If I call you names, is that as harmful as if I punch you?

We have so far discussed how *I* would like to live, as an individual. What, however, about those around me. Should decisions on what is a good life be taken at the individual level – what *I* want, what *I* need – or should we be thinking at a communal level – what *we* want, what *we* need.

Imagine I live by a river. This is very convenient for me because I can conduct crazy experiments and dump all the resulting chemicals into the river. The chemicals just magically disappear with the current. I wash myself, go to the bathroom, and the river just takes it all away. But a little bit further down the river, there is another family. And they are getting all my contaminated water. So, they come to visit me and ask if I could find a way to live that did not result in my dirty water flowing down to them. I tell them I will think about it. As I sit here thinking about it, with my feet dangling in my river water, suddenly I see some trash float down to me. What? Disgusting! What is that?!! I run upriver and find that another family has moved there. And they are now using the river as they please.

We have two options here. Each individual/family can keep doing what they want, passing the dirt downriver, or we can come up with a communal option, a way to live that considers everyone, not just the individual or individual family.

To think communally means, at least in some ways, limiting what you want. For example, if you come across a plate of delicious, melt-in-your mouth chocolate chip cookies, you might want to eat all the cookies … but you are going to stop yourself to ensure your friends/family can also get some.

All for Us, None for You

This could be taken to an extreme. Living in a way that makes others happy but leaves you with no space for your own wishes would be asphyxiating. There are lots of stories and books that explore the idea of the individual being sacrificed for the good of society. In the novel *We* by Russian author Yevgeny Zamyatin, individuals have no choices, and even their emotions are taken away, so that the community can live in harmony. People are given numbers instead of names to avoid creating individuality.

During the Cold War the Soviet Union was presented as an example of a society where the individual was completely sacrificed for the wellbeing of the group.[4] Everyone got the same, no individuality was allowed. The USA, on the other hand, was presented as a place where individuals were completely selfish, thinking only about what they wanted even if this hurt their community and their loved ones.[5] Both depictions were exaggerations. The Soviet Union was a failed attempt to try and force communism[6] and it had plenty of selfish individualism. The USA on the other hand had some very selfish individuals, but also many who worked hard to advance the wellbeing of communities.

Extremes are usually not good. But reaching a golden middle, a place where we can be both individuals *and* community members, where we can be free to creatively pursue our unique interests *and* also consider and support the wellbeing of others (which might require us to limit our own freedoms) is hard.

Looking at Global Issues – Ecuador

The struggle between what *you* want/need and what *others* want/need is also a global struggle. If every country does whatever it wants, it impacts other countries. If a country, for example, chooses to burn all its fossil fuel, to cut down all its trees and cover every square inch of its land with concrete … its poor choices will not just affect its citizens. When carbon dioxide pollutes the air and heat radiates from the paved ground, it will affect the whole planet.

The reason for this, as you know, is that we live in a global ecosystem. Pollution caused in one area of the world does not stay there, it spreads through water, air, and soil. If a country chooses to live in a way that is destructive, we all suffer. The opposite is also the case, if a country helps maintain forests and jungles, if a country keeps pollutants out of the water, air, and soil, we all benefit.

But should a country be concerned with the wellbeing of the world, or just of its own citizens? If my country finds oil in its territory this could mean great wealth for my citizens! The money from the oil could build hospitals, feed children, increase education … should I keep my citizens poor just so the rest of the world can benefit?

This is what happened in Ecuador. Ecuador has incredible biodiversity. It also has oil and a tremendous amount of poverty. If Ecuador exploits its oil, it could make a lot of money and feed its citizens. However, in the process, it would destroy one of the most important rainforests in the world. The destruction of the rainforest is not just a loss for Ecuador, it is a loss for the world.

With this in mind, the government of Ecuador came up with a proposal. What if Ecuador keep the oil underground, left the rainforest untouched for the benefit of the whole world and, in exchange, countries paid Ecuador some of the value of the oil Ecuador could have taken out and sold. This was a win-win situation, argued Ecuador. Everyone gets a healthier planet, an untouched rainforest, and Ecuador gets the money it needs.

Would you have supported Ecuador's request?

Sadly, the support needed for this project did not come about. Other countries argued that they should not have to pay Ecuador to make the right choice. They further argued that they should not take money from their citizens to pay for the wellbeing of Ecuador's citizens.

Ecuador pointed out that rich countries, like the UK and the USA, became wealthy by creating a lot of pollution in the past (and in the present), and it is hypocritical and unfair to now tell poor countries that they should not pollute. The rich countries, now with money, should put their money where their mouth is, so to say, and help poor countries make the right choice for the benefit of everyone. When Ecuador did not receive the money it asked for, Ecuador's president decided that the wellbeing of Ecuador's citizens took precedence over environmental concerns, and opted to start oil drilling.

Here we are back to the questions we started this chapter with, but at the level of a country. What is a good life for a country, or what is the right way for a country to develop? Should a country be free to follow its interests, even if it costs the planet, or should a country think about the safety of the world, of humans in other countries? Should a country sacrifice its present enjoyment (for example of the stuff they can get by exploiting oil) for the sake of our future wellbeing (so that we do not cook in an overheated planet)?

Changing Economic Policies – Degrowth

In the twenty-first century most people think a country is doing well when it is growing: more jobs, more production, more money. Their citizens can eat more, travel, buy. This is often seen as a good life for a country.

However, a group of economic and political philosophers, such as Latouche, Ilich, and Kallis, have asked countries to consider *degrowth*. The idea of degrowth is that countries should produce less, consume less, use less. This is the opposite of what most countries are trying to do!

Advocates of degrowth note that making and using more things uses up natural resources and creates pollution. We simply cannot keep producing more and more. We are not only running out of the ingredients we need to produce more things, but we are also creating more and more trash which kills animals and plants. The production and transportation processes impact our planet by creating green gases which trap heat and lead to global warming.

So, perhaps we should produce less, consume less, waste less. However, choosing what to stop producing is not easy. What should we produce less of? Food? Clothes? Even if you shut down a factory that makes something quite unnecessary – an umbrella for squirrels, for example – you are limiting the choices of the people that wanted to buy these umbrellas and chase squirrels with them. And closing this factory will leave some people unemployed, limiting their freedom to eat, making them less safe.

Moreover, the reality is that we have gotten used to living with lots of things. A lot of people, for example, have several pairs of shoes, even while many around the world own no shoes, or maybe only one pair. But if you are used to having many things, having less can feel like a loss of choices, of freedom.

Degrowth, then, can be argued to limit freedom: freedom to produce and freedom to consume, to have. But it can also be argued that degrowth is giving us more freedom: freedom to live into the future, with clean air and biodiversity. Freedom to survive.

You might feel that asking a country to produce less is harming you. It limits your choices, your options. But continuing to produce as much as we do is also harming our environment. So how do we decide which harm is more serious?

Clearly choosing a good life for a country is just as challenging as choosing a good life for an individual.

Conclusion

You are back in the contest to choose your perfect life. You can open a magical door and, as you step through it, enter the perfect life you will live forever – well, until you die. Except now, as you make this choice, you have more to think about. You have a more complex understanding of what freedom is and requires – each person's freedom requires limiting other people's freedom. And to be free you need resources and support – so maybe you can't just be free on your own. Complete freedom would mean no safety, the constant threat of harm. Is it worth it? You have also thought about how your actions might affect others – both your community and other countries.

So, what do you think is a good life?

Even if you are not sure what to choose, the fact that you are thinking about it means you are in good company. Socrates, the father of Western philosophy, famously said, 'The unexamined life is not worth living'. This is at the core of political and moral philosophy: examining our lives and thinking about how we live. And to do so, Ptahhotep, an ancient Egyptian thinker, reminds us that we need to be humble, and learn from others.

Chapter Summary

In this chapter we have considered what is 'a good life'. We have started to think about what freedom is and what it requires. We have considered how an individual's freedom, or a country's freedom, will affect others. We have thought a bit about economic choices and their impact and have also thought about our impact on the environment. We have encountered Nietzsche's ideas of eternal reoccurrence – life repeating itself in a loop, J. S. Mill's harm principle, and Isaiah Berlin's ideas of positive and negative freedoms. You were also briefly introduced to degrowth ideas, which can be linked back to Ivan Illich and Serge Latouche as well André Gorz, and Nicholas Georgescu-Roegen. Feel free to research them further.

Freedom is complicated. Would you give some freedom up for the wellbeing of others? Would you value safety above freedom? Or would you rather avoid both questions and plug yourself into a computer game? Remember, whatever you choose, Nietzsche challenges you to live it again and again … forever.

Pondering Points

- What do you think is more important for a good life: freedom or security?
- Think about your country. Does your country prioritise freedom or security? Can you think of a country that values the opposite?
- Do you think what you value in life changes as you age? For example, do you think a toddler might think freedom the most important thing, while an adult might value security more?

References

Associated Press. "Yasuni: Ecuador Abandons Plan to Stave Off Amazon Drilling." *The Guardian*, August 16, 2013. www.theguardian.com/world/2013/aug/16/ecuador-abandons-yasuni-amazon-drilling.

Ball, Terence, and Richard Dagger. *Political Ideologies and the Democratic Ideal*. New York: Pearson, 2020.

Berlin, Isaiah. "Two Concepts of Liberty." In *Four Essays on Liberty*, 118–172. Oxford: Oxford University Press, 1969.

Conquest, Robert. *The Great Terror: A Reassessment*. New York: Oxford University Press, 1990.

Illich, Ivan. *Tools for Conviviality*. New York: Harper & Row, 1973.

Kallis, Giorgos. *Degrowth*. United Kingdom: Agenda Publishing, 2018.

Lasch, Christopher. *The Culture of Narcissism: American Life in an Age of Diminishing Expectations*. New York: W.W. Norton & Company, 1979.

Latouche, Serge. *Farewell to Growth*. Cambridge, MA: Polity Press, 2009.

Mill, John Stuart. *On Liberty*. Edited by Elizabeth Rapaport. Indianapolis: Hackett Publishing Company, 1978.

Nietzsche, Friedrich. *The Gay Science: With a Prelude in Rhymes and an Appendix of Songs*. Translated by Walter Kaufmann. New York: Vintage Books, 1974.

Open Case Studies. *Yasuní-ITT Initiative: Protecting Biodiversity and Indigenous Rights in Ecuador*. University of British Columbia. www.cases.open.ubc.ca/yesuni-itt-initiative-protecting-biodiversity-and-indigenous-rights-in-ecuador/. (Accessed June 27, 2024).

Plato. "Apology." In *Five Dialogues*, translated by G.M.A. Grube, revised by John M. Cooper, 2nd ed. Indianapolis: Hackett Publishing Company, 2002.

Press Association. "Court Rules Woman Can Keep Her Red and White Striped Townhouse." *The Guardian*, April 24, 2017. www.theguardian.com/uk-news/2017/apr/24/red-white-striped-house-zipporah-lisle-mainwaring.

Ptahhotep. "The Instructions of Ptahhotep." In *The Literature of Ancient Egypt: An Anthology of Stories, Instructions, Stelae, Autobiographies, and Poetry*, edited by William Kelly Simpson, translated by Zbyněk Žába, 129–148, 3rd ed. New Haven: Yale University Press, 2003.

Yale E360. "Wealthy Nations Overstating Climate Aid, Report Finds." *Yale Environment 360*, June 5, 2023. www.e360.yale.edu/digest/climate-finance-aid-donor-funds.

Zamyatin, Yevgeny. *We*. Translated by Clarence Brown. New York: Penguin Books, 1993.

6 Who Makes You, You?

Discussing Identity

If we are going to make the world a better place, perhaps we should start by thinking about the people and communities that make up this world. Humans. You and me. What are we like? What makes us who we are?

'Let me propose a story to think about who we are', Thomas Hobbes interjects to the party guests. 'Imagine we go sailing around the world. We travel on a large, wooden ship, named 'BoatyMcBoatface' with enough supplies for many months at sea. The journey is hard on the ship: storms, salt water, the weight of the crew, passengers, supplies ... As the days go on, some of the ship's boards brake, some rot. Each is carefully replaced by another. Its screws oxidize, they are replaced. The boat stays afloat, and the voyage continues. Many moons later, the boat returns to its home. Every single one of its planks, and all of its metal parts, have been replaced during the voyage. Is the ship that returns home the same ship as the one that we sailed off in?'

The thought experiment Hobbes is presenting is known as the Ship of Theseus.[1] Since every single part of the ship has been replaced, is it a new ship? If it is a different ship, when did it become so? When the first board was replaced? When more than half of its parts had been replaced? When were all new? The overall question is what makes this Boaty McBoatface, Boaty McBoatface? Is it its component parts, or the combination of these? Or its experiences? Its journey?

The larger question is what gives something its identity? We can apply this thought experiment to ourselves. Are we the sum of our individual cells, or are we somehow more than the sum of these small parts? When your cells die and are replaced by new cells – is that a new you?

DOI: 10.4324/9781032620121-8

You.exe

Could you be made into a digital file? Could everything that is you be made into data that can be downloaded and uploaded to replicate you? If so, what would this file, 'you.exe', contain? Your eye colour, your voice, your sense of humour, the books you have read, the smell of your feet?

Assuming we can get all this data, if we then download this data into another human body, would that be you?

Imagine looking out of different eyes, looking down at different hands that move when you think of using your fingers. A body that is not the one you have always been in. Would you still be you? How much of yourself, or your sense of self, is contained in your body?

This question is particularly relevant to people who donate or receive organs. If there is a part of you that is in your heart, will that part of you always be with the person who receives your heart? Will the person whose heart is replaced, on the other hand, be somehow missing a part of who they are?

To what extent we are our bodies is much more urgent when we discuss more visible changes and organ donations. For example, people who have had catastrophic accidents sometimes require a face transplant.[2] The face of a person who has died is grafted onto their skull. After surgery, once swelling has gone down, they will be looking at a face that is not the face they were born with – it is also not quite the face of the donor, as the skin adapts to the patients' bone structure. Seeing yourself with a new face is not an easy thing. Psychologists need to help those undergoing this procedure before, during, and after the surgery, as they learn to see themselves in a new face. Patients must come to terms with looking differently and consider how this makes them feel about who they are.

If we change our face, are we a different person? Or the same person with a new face? If we can be the same person with a new face, does this mean that our body does not matter in terms of who we are, or that it is just one component of what makes us, us?

You Can Never Step Into the Same River Twice

Pre-Socratic philosopher Heraclitus once said 'You can never step into the same river twice'. What did he mean? If you go kayaking in a river on Monday, and go back on Friday, the river is still there. Same river, same name, same location. However, if you think about it, it is not the same river. The molecules of water that make up that river are moving. Some are being swept down current, some are evaporating, some are being soaked into the ground, or absorbed by plants, some are drunk by animals. The fish that live in the river are swimming to different places. Some are being eaten by other fish. Other animals visit the river. New insects and animals are born in/on the water. Over decades, the river will cut new paths into the ground, create canyons, or perhaps break into two. Thus, every time we step into the river, even if we step into the exact same location, we are surrounded by different water, by different living forms. Every moment in time, the river has changed.

What if we are the same way? We know that our cells are constantly changing – dying and being replaced with new cells. So, in a biological way, you are not the same person you were when you were two. Biologically this is obvious – you are much taller than you were at two! Besides getting taller your brain has gone through tremendous growth, with hormonal changes affecting your development, allowing you to think and feel differently than you did as a toddler. Are you the same person, now, as you were then? Or are you a different version of the same person?

Of course, you have not changed just biologically. You have experienced many new things since you were two. You have probably lost a whole set of teeth and learnt to speak. You have watched hundreds of hours of television and read millions of words. You have many more ideas to use in your thoughts. If you have lived through war, or a traumatic event, these experiences would have further affected you.

Each person changes not just biologically, in terms of cells and hormones, but also emotionally and psychologically, given what they experience. When we talk about who we are, therefore, perhaps it is difficult to think of ourselves as a single entity. Maybe we are like a river – the same but always different. Buddha would agree with this view, as Buddhist philosophy thinks that the idea of self is an illusion. We are constantly changing.

Being in the Twenty-First Century

Trying to figure out who we are in the present has challenges our ancestors did not encounter. Imagine for example, growing up before there were mirrors. Sure, you might catch a glimpse of yourself in water, or maybe on some polished metal, but it would be a blurry image. And it would not be something you can see every day, and much less multiple times a day.

In contrast, think about how many times most people see themselves now. There are mirrors and reflective surfaces everywhere. As you walk around, your image is constantly reflected at you on windows, shop surfaces, CCTV cameras, smart phones. And we are now able to take pictures of ourselves constantly. And these are not blurry, vague pictures. Cameras can zoom in to give us almost microscopic images of our faces – making us aware of details – the size and location of each of our pores – our ancestors might have never considered.

Cameras and lights, however, can also give us a distorted reflection of who we are. We can freeze odd expressions that last only a microsecond into pictures that can be shared forever. We can alter images to give us a false sense of what we and others look like. French Philosopher Jean Baudrillard discusses how technology can blur the distinction between reality and fiction. In social media we can present different versions of ourselves – editing photos to make us look thoughtful, or silly, or adventurous. But how can we distinguish these fictional versions of ourselves and others from the 'real' person? Does the 'real' person exist, or are we just a composite creation of what we present to others?

We live in a world of true and false mirrors. Trying to figure out who we are in the midst of all these false and blurry images is hard.

Are You Who You Say, Or Who I Say?

Deciding who you are is also in part deciding who you are not. Identities are built by exclusion. Think about national identities. If you are British, you are not French, or German, or Japanese. National identities are built by borders. Cross a border and you are in a different country, with different rules, with, the argument goes, different people.

But this gets difficult. What if you see yourself in a different way from how others see you? Whose views count when it comes to who you are? What if you think of yourself as Colombian, but everyone thinks of you as French? Maybe you were born in Colombia have Colombian parents, but have lived in Paris since you were 1, and speak Spanish with a French accent. When you visit Colombia people say you are French – but you are Colombian, you say! Is the way you see yourself more or less important than how others see you?

Of course, this could be a false dichotomy. The idea that you have to be either this or that, could be wrong. Why can't you be two things at once? You could be both British and French. You can be happy and sad. In terms of nationalities, in some countries you can have dual nationality – you can have a US citizenship *and* an Italian citizenship, for example. In terms of politics, however, this can be problematic. If you are part of country A and B and these countries go to war, which side will you support?

Some philosophers, such as Judith Butler, see identity as something you perform. You act in a way that fits what that identity is supposed to be. If you are French, for example, you would speak French, eat cheese and baguettes. Wear a beret. 'That is a ridiculous cartoon of what being French is!' I can hear you muttering. This is true. Of course, being French can be none of these things, all or some of them, depending on the particular French person you meet. The thing with identities, however, is that they are in part a bit like acting roles, which you have to fulfil to be seen as participating in the identity. An identity is something that is created in interaction with others – how you present yourself to them, and how they see you. To what extent you fit the list of what that identity is supposed to be.

Another example is gender. Some might think that to be a girl you have to like pink, want long hair, draw flowers in all your things, and prefer making cakes to doing sport. But, of course, many, many girls like none of those things.

Some girls like boxing, hate pink, like short hair and prefer to climb mountains or play videogames rather than bake. There is no recipe for how to be 'a girl', or 'a French person', but it seems like humans like to build boxes of what these identities should be – as these boxes help us understand our world – and then we try to force people into them. And being forced to be something you are not can hurt.

It can also be painful if someone tries to erase who you are. This has been the case for indigenous peoples. When Europeans took over what is now the Americas and started new countries they did not want to have the identities of indigenous peoples as part of the new countries. This was in part because it was difficult to build a sense of unity with multiple identities, but it was also in part because they saw the culture and language of indigenous people as inferior. And they did not want to acknowledge that something was already there, in the 'new' country they were starting. Therefore, they tried to erase indigenous identities by prohibiting their languages and traditions. For some people holding on to their identity or the identity of their ancestors is an attempt to rebuild a sense of self that was hurt by colonial processes. Imagine if someone came to your house, burned all your family albums, changed your name and made you learn a new language. When you could, would you not want to remember your family, your history, your past?

How Do You Know You Are?

Perhaps before even discussing what makes you, you, we should ask: how do you even know that you are?

You think you are reading this book now but, what if it is just a dream? What if you have imagined this book, this chapter, this page?

You drop the book and look around. There are things around you. Your room. You can smell dinner. You can hear birds and cars outside.

But, again, how do you know any of what your senses tell you is real. What if everything that is happening is an illusion … a trick being played on you by someone?

This is René Descartes' thought experiment. Descartes wanted to create a system of thought that did not assume anything – a system of thought based only on things we could prove and be certain about. We cannot *know* that things around us exist. If you have ever dreamt or hallucinated, you know you can firmly believe in the existence of things that actually do not exist. In one of my dreams my dog and I shared a pizza and chatted about cats. During the dream I was 100% convinced my dog was a witty conversationalist who could use a fork and knife. In real life … he just drools.

If we cannot trust what we think we see/hear/taste … then, Descartes asked, how can know that we exist? How can we know we are real?

Descartes came up with a clever solution. There is much you cannot prove as real. You cannot know that you have hands, or that you come from a particular country. You cannot know that your dog has never made knock-knock jokes … But even as you think about what you do not know, you can *know* that you are thinking. The fact that you are thinking proves that you exist. If we did not exist, we could not be thinking about whether we exist. If we are thinking, we exist. And so, Descartes came up with one of the most famous phrases in philosophy: *I think, therefore, I am*, or in Latin – *Cogito ergo sum*.

You Are What You Do

Existentialist philosophers, such as Jean-Paul Sartre argue that who we are is up to us. It is up to what we do. It is your actions that determine who you are. If you say you are a painter, but in fact never pick up a crayon, a paintbrush, or a coloured pencil in your life, are you really a painter? If you say you are a kind person, but yell at whoever walks in front of you and pull the whiskers of kittens, are you really?

In other words, who you are is up to you. You exist, but who are you? Your essence is up to you. This is a great freedom. It is also a great responsibility. For some, this might seem terrifying. It is up to you to decide who you are. You can become a thinker, a creator, a healer … or you can become a thief, a destroyer. You could become simply what others tell you you are. Or worse yet, you could become nothing. Leave the world without making any difference. It is up to you.

Memories

If you make up who you are by doing things, then what would happen if you forgot everything you ever did? Imagine waking up tomorrow with no memories at all.

Imagine you are walking down the road one stormy day. Suddenly the air gets cold, the sky turns steely blue and … you are hit by lightning! Incredibly, other than pushing you to the ground and frying your hair into a crazy perm, the lightening does not hurt you. But when you open your eyes and peel yourself off the pavement, you realise the lighting has somehow created a carbon copy of you. Next to you is someone who is identical to you … except they don't have any of your memories. Is this person, you? Or are they simply someone who *could* have been you – if they had your experiences?

If our memories are the key to who we are, does this mean that if we can transfer your memories, all of them, to a new body, it would be you? This takes us back to the idea of downloading who you are. It can also take us back to our thought experiment of the Ship of Theseus. Perhaps what makes the ship the same ship is not what planks it is made from, but the fact that all the people on the ship shared the memories of the voyage. It is their memories, rather than anything physical, that gives that ship its identity.

One way to think about identities and memories is to think about how national identities are made (such as the Japanese, the Ghanian, the American identity).[3] Sociologist Benedict Anderson argued that nations are 'imagined communities'. In other words, nations are not natural things – like volcanoes – which exist whether humans know they are there or not. A nation is something we construct by imagining it. We imagine things like stories, and music, and traditions and share these with each other. And we share memories. Think about what Americans use to build up the idea of what it is to be American. This might vary depending on what part of the USA you are in, but it is likely to include the national anthem, the flag, stories about the Boston Tea Party, the Wild West, the Declaration of Independence, Paul Revere riding through the night, Thanksgiving ... Now think about what makes up the idea of being British. Again, this will vary but might include tea and scones, the Tower of London, Stonehenge, Waterloo, Churchill and WWII, the Royal Family, Paddington Bear.

Of course, in the building of each nation we remember some things and forget others. In the making of the idea of the USA, for example, the violence native Americans were made to suffer is often forgotten. Thanksgiving is often remembered as a time of sharing and gratitude ... but the betrayal of those indigenous people who helped is forgotten. Slavery is remembered in part, but its consequences are often dismissed. Similarly, when thinking about what it is to be British, the Troubles with Ireland are rarely mentioned, as is the mistreatment of the Windrush generation. Communities have selective memory – and selective amnesia.

How should countries choose what they remember and what they forget? This is clearly at least in part an issue of power. The memories of the most powerful are put up in walls, the memories of those defeated are erased. What one studies in school as history is part of how we build our collective memories of who we were and who we are. Fights over history are not just an academic issue, they are about building an identity that includes or excludes certain stories, and with those stories, certain people.

Should we remember bad memories? As a person, you might not want to remember traumatic or even embarrassing memories – like that time you ran into a glass door like a fly in front of your friends. But then, aren't even your worst memories part of what makes you, you? What you experienced helps you understand others. Does it not work in a similar way for communities? Should countries forget wars they fought, or crimes they committed?

How to deal with bad memories is not a simple thing. People have access to therapy. What can a country access to heal itself? After a civil war, for example, when a country has been divided and citizens have killed each other, will remembering the violence build anger and resentment that might result in new violence? On the other hand, can the past be forgotten, or will it always come back to haunt us until we make peace with it? If we forget the past, will we repeat it?

All cultures have some sort of ceremony to deal with death, to mourn, to let go of the dead so the living can keep living. But if a country has not acknowledged those killed in its past, perhaps the living cannot move on?

Conclusion

Have you decided what it is that makes you, you? Is it your memories, your body, your unique way of thinking, what you do, or a combination of all of these? Or are you something more than any of these, something that is changing and being re-made every day? To what extent is who you are a result of where you live, of what communities you are a part of, of the way others see you?

If there is one thing I am certain of, it is that each of us, individually, and each community we are a part of, is an incredible, complex, and fascinating universe. Getting to know ourselves is a life-long journey. In ancient Greece 'Know thyself' was inscribed at the Temple of Apollo at Delphi. Getting to know ourselves is not easy, but the more we learn about who we are, the more we can also start to understand and be kind to others, as we realise that despite our different histories, we share our common humanity.

Chapter Summary

In this chapter we have discussed what it is that makes us who we are. By starting with a discussion of organ donations, we have looked at our individual identity and discussed whether our bodies, our minds, our emotions, our memories, our actions, or a combination of these is what makes us who we are. We have discussed whether who we are is permanent, or whether a permanent identity is a delusion, as Buddah argued, and our identity is always changing like Heraclitus' river. We discussed whether we decide who we are, whether we 'act' who we are, or perform it as philosopher Judith Butler called it, or whether culture and societies try to put us into boxes of what we are supposed to be. We discuss the impact of modernity in how we build ourselves, and how technology can create hyperreality, as discussed by Jean Baudrillar, where we struggle to separate our real self from the fictional representations we create online.

We have also noted that some identities have been ignored, mistreated, or even erased in history, and considered what impact this has for individuals.

Pondering Points

- Imagine an evil philosopher switches your brain with that of another person. Now your brain is in their body and their brain is in your body. The evil philosopher then says, 'Don't worry, I will not hurt you, but I must hurt your friend, just tell me who you are, and I will not hurt you'.

Who are you? Your brain in your friend's body or your body with your friend's brain?

- If you were put in charge of creating a museum for a country after a civil war, and both sides in the war want their heroes to have statues in the museum, would you allow this?
- Now you are creating the museum of YOU. You must choose three things to represent you for eternity. What would these be?

References

Anderson, Benedict. *Imagined Communities: Reflections on the Origin and Spread of Nationalism*. London: Verso, 1983.

Azevedo, Ruben T., J. Rodrigo Diaz-Siso, Allyson R. Alfonso, Elie P. Ramly, Rami S. Kantar, Zoe P. Berman, Gustave K. Diep, William J. Rifkin, Eduardo D. Rodriguez, and Manos Tsakiris. "Re-cognizing the New Self: The Neurocognitive Plasticity of Self-Processing Following Facial Transplantation." *Proceedings of the National Academy of Sciences* 120, no. 14 (March 27, 2023): e2211966120. https://doi.org/10.1073/pnas.2211966120.

Barth, Fredrik. *Ethnic Groups and Boundaries: The Social Organization of Culture Difference*. Boston: Little, Brown and Company, 1969.

Baudrillard, Jean. "Simulacra and Simulations." In *Selected Writings*, edited by Mark Poster, 166–184. Stanford, CA: Stanford University Press, 1988.

Butler, Judith. *Gender Trouble: Feminism and the Subversion of Identity*. New York: Routledge, 1990.

Descartes, René. *Discourse on the Method*. Translated by Ian Maclean. Edited by David Weissman. Indianapolis: Hackett Publishing Company, 1998.

Harvey, Peter. *The Selfless Mind: Personality, Consciousness and Nirvana in Early Buddhism*. Richmond: Curzon Press, 1995.

Heraclitus. *Fragments*. Translated by T. M. Robinson. Toronto: University of Toronto Press, 1987.

Plutarch. "Life of Theseus." In *Parallel Lives*, translated by Bernadotte Perrin, Vol. 1. Cambridge, MA: Harvard University Press, 1914.

Poole, Ross. "Memory, History and the Claims of the Past." *Memory Studies* 1, no. 2 (2008): 149–166. https://doi.org/10.1177/1750698007088383.

Sartre, Jean-Paul. *Being and Nothingness: An Essay on Phenomenological Ontology*. Translated by Hazel E. Barnes. New York: Philosophical Library, 1956.

Smiles, Deondre. "Erasing Indigenous History, Then and Now." *Origins: Current Events in Historical Perspective*. www.origins.osu.edu/article/erasing-indigenous-history-then-and-now?language_content_entity=en. (Accessed June 27, 2024).

7   Why Do We Go to War?

Discussing Human Nature and International Relations

In the last chapter, we considered human nature. Whether we are made up by our biology, our culture, our actions. Previously we considered what a good way to live would be.

In our imaginary philosophers' party Thomas Hobbes has a lot to say about both topics. 'If this party had no rules', he claims, 'some of you might attack me and try to eat my food. You might even kill me to get the largest slice of cake, which I got!' he pauses to take a bite. 'It is human nature!'. He takes another huge bite.

Neil Noddings, one of the key philosophers of the ethics of care, strongly disagrees 'I doubt so! Humans are not vultures! If someone attacked you, we would defend you and care for you. Humans care for each other, don't attack each other over a piece of cake!'

'You are mistaken there, madam, humans are innately self-interested! Without a higher power, humans descend into war and violence!' Now chocolate cake is flying out of Hobbes mouth as he gets animated.

Locke jumps in 'Surely humans are what they are taught to be. Each child is born as a tabula rasa – a blank slate – to be filled with education. And there is such a thing as natural law. We don't just go around hurting each other!'

Hobbes scoffs, 'You cannot educate the human out of their nature! Only threats keep us from fighting over resources, or honour, or cake!'.

I wonder what threats Hobbes think I am using to keep philosophers from fighting over the chocolate cake?

Humans in Space

The year is 3057. Humanity is looking for a new planet to inhabit. A rocket with 50 explorers from around the world is sent out toward Mars. On their way there, unexplained cosmic forces derail the rocket. The explorers are launched into

DOI: 10.4324/9781032620121-9

unknown territory. Soon they lose all communication with Earth. Miraculously the explorers find an uncharted dwarf planet. They decide to land on this planet using up most of their fuel.

The planet is thick with luscious plants the explorers have never seen before. There are some fluorescent berries that taste like chocolate and seem to give those who eat them superhuman strength! There are also a variety of animals, some of which are clearly dangerous, and some of which might be eaten for food. Crucially, the planet has an atmosphere humans can live in. Humans can survive here! But they are too far from Earth to make contact or to return.
What do you think will happen with this group of explorers?

Do you think:

Scenario 1 – They will work together to start a small, peaceful society, that survives for generations.[1]

Scenario 2 – Tensions within the group will emerge. There will be fights about who is in charge and what the survival strategy should be. Some want to look for a way to contact Earth and leave the planet, even if not everyone can leave. There will be fights over food distribution and how to guard against predators. Some explorers will choose violence to get themselves – and those who support them – all the super-strength berries. Other explorers will start to sharpen spears to defend themselves and guard the food. Some explorers may get hurt and even killed. The group will split into factions and people live in stress, constantly looking over their shoulder, afraid of being attacked by other factions. Only a few will survive, in an increasingly savage way.

Which scenario do you think is most likely?

Sixteenth-century philosopher Thomas Hobbes would argue for the second scenario.[2] Hobbes believed that without rules and a ruler to enforce these rules, men will fight. First, they will fight for resources. If there are limited fluorescent berries to eat in this planet, explorers will fight over who gets the berries. A group will start hoarding berries. Another group will argue they deserve more because they work harder/are older/are smarter …

Even if there is no competition for food or shelter, however, Hobbes argues that men will still fight. They will fight for honour. One of the explorers may feel insulted and seek revenge. Somebody else thinks they should be the leader and starts plotting a take-over. Humans, according to Hobbes, are always looking for power. Without rules to stop them, they will stop at nothing to gain power.

According to Hobbes, human nature in a state of nature, that is in a state without rules, will result in violence. As each person seeks their own interests, there will be constant fights and more and more violence. Everyone will fight everyone else – it will be war of all against all: *Bellum omnium contra omnes*. Life in such a state, Hobbes argues, would be awful: 'No arts; no letters; no society; and which is worst of all, continual fear and danger of violent death; and the life of man, solitary, poor, nasty, brutish, and short' (Hobbes 1651, Pt 1, Ch 13).

Of course: if all around you is violence and fear, you will not have time to learn or do anything beautiful, and you will likely die soon.

Now, imagine if one of the explorers had a weapon and the ability to punish anyone who threatened others. According to Hobbes, order would then be kept. Of course, the explorers would not be free to do whatever they wanted. The explorers would be giving up some of their freedom in exchange for being safe.[3] But it makes sense – rather lose some freedom than lose your life.

Do you think Hobbes is correct? Will humans become violent and fight if there are no threatening rulers to keep them in line?

Think about what you have experienced. If you start playing football with a few other people, but there is no one to enforce any rules, is it likely that some of the players might start bending the rules to gain more points? Would you need a referee to ensure no one 'accidentally' pushes another player?

Are Countries Like People?

Let's use Hobbes' theory about human nature to think about countries. Here you have country A, let's call it Amazonia, which has a great amount of oil under its soil. And country B, let's call it Brockia, which would quite like to have that oil for its own citizens. What prevents Brockia from attacking Amazonia and taking it over, or at least taking its oil?

If we use Hobbes' logic, countries are like explorers in a planet – they are each out for their own survival. It is a state of nature. There is no one to enforce rules. Some countries might try to work together and agree that attacking each other for their resources, such as oil, is not nice. But some countries might think playing nice is for wimps and choose to attack even if their actions are frowned upon by other countries (looking at you, Stalin). Some countries might start looking around for sharp sticks, or nuclear weapons, to defend themselves or to scare others from attacking them.

In real life, there is no 'world police', there is no global army that will step in to stop Brockia from attacking Amazonia. It is possible that other countries might come together and defend Amazonia in case of an attack. But they might not. They might decide defending Amazonia is not worth the death of their own people. Or they might decide it is more important to stay on the good side of Brockia.

If you were the president of Amazonia, what would you do?

You might try and build allegiances with other countries. But these could fail. Or Brockia could build its own allegiances and then you would have a bigger enemy to face.

Weapons. You need to arm yourself. To be ready to defend yourself. Hopefully, you will never need to use these weapons because the sole fact of having them will scare others from attacking you. Will Brockia attack Amazonia if Amazonia has nuclear weapons? Not likely.

But then Brockia and other countries might start to worry that Amazonia with its nuclear weapons will attack them. They need to get their own weapons.

What we have now is an arms race. Maybe this is why so many countries spend a good portion of their income on weapons.

If we follow Hobbes' logic that humans are self-interested and kept from violence only by harshly imposed rules, and assume that countries are like humans – each interested in their own survival and glory, with no global ruler to stop them from violence – then the world is an inevitably violent place, and war will occur. This is a *realist* theory of international relations. The only way to prevent a war is to arm yourself enough to scare others from attacking you. If there are several big countries with lots of weapons, the world might be in a 'balance of power'. In this balance no one attacks because they know they can be attacked back. It is not violent, it is stable, but it is dangerous and depends on staying armed, ready to fight, and maintaining the balance – if anyone gets a new weapon, the balance is gone.

Was Hobbes Right?

You might have come across plenty of books and movies that build on Hobbes' ideas – *Lord of the Flies* by William Golding is one of the most famous. A group of boys is stranded on an island with no rules and – spoiler alert – *bellum omnium contra omnes*. Stories like *Lord of the Flies* imagine scenarios where all rules are gone, and chaos erupts as each self-interested person does whatever they needed to do for *número uno* – for themselves.

But, was Hobbes right?

In 1965 a group of young teen boys from Tonga decided they were tired of their school meals and 'borrowed' a ship for a quick fishing adventure. However, a storm ripped their ship to pieces, and they found themselves stranded on a tiny island. Six boys, no rules, and only whatever food they could hunt and gather with only one knife. What do you think happened?

Months went by. Back home, the boys' families assumed they were dead, conducted their funerals, and mourned their loss. Then one day a fishing boat saw the signs of a fire on a deserted island and realised someone was there. To the huge surprise of everyone, the boys returned home safe.

After over a year, no one had expected these boys to be alive. Much less did they expect them to have created a small garden, to have found and re-domesticated chickens, to have even created a small gym where they all worked out. They had also built and tended a fire the whole time they were there, in the hope that a ship would see it and come to their rescue.

These six boys proved Hobbes wrong. They survived through cooperation and kindness. In the 15 months they lived on the island no violent state of nature emerged. At one point one of the boys fell off a cliff and broke his leg. The other boys carried him to safety, set his leg, and took care of him while he healed.

Maybe violence and war are not an inevitable part of human nature. Maybe kindness and cooperation can create peaceful societies. Maybe countries can cooperate and work for the wellbeing of humanity, rather than just their own citizens.

John Locke disagreed with Hobbes. He argued that there is a law of nature: humans naturally want to avoid hurting others. We naturally recognise that fellow humans, as creatures of God, have the right to be free, to live, to pursue happiness. Based on Locke's ideas, a *liberal* theory of international relations argues for the creation of organisations that foster cooperation between states – such as the United Nations. Realist, however, agree with Hobbes and think the best foreign policy is one of military preparation as the world is in anarchy: there are no rules.

Nature Versus Nurture

Perhaps Hobbes was wrong in his understanding of human nature. Perhaps it is our upbringing that has made us aggressive, competitive, afraid. That is, maybe it is nurture, not nature, that Hobbes is writing about. Humans are competitive if they are in a situation where success can only come from putting others down. For example, if only one student in your class can get the top prize, there is no incentive to collaborate with others. If you find a way to study more, faster, you will keep this information to yourself.

If our society was different, however, perhaps humans would grow up to be different. The cooperative side of our nature could be developed. When you see someone suffering, you would be inspired to help, not to take their money and walk away fast.

Some philosophers, such as Nel Noddings, argue that caring is an innate part of human nature. From birth we depend on others. Humans are interdependent. Our species has survived because we care for others – the elderly, children, the ill, even when they can do nothing to advance our interests. We are not driven just by competition. We have empathy and compassion for others.[4]

This could be a cultural issue. Hobbes was looking at the world from his own perspective. He was living through a Civil War. This was a period of great violence as different groups sought power. Perhaps Hobbes thought that every man was born seeking power, and that life was full of dangers and fear because that is what he saw around him. It is easy to think that our reality is all reality. If we are in war, we think everyone is always in war.

A Matter of Numbers?

Then again, maybe it is not about human nature or cultures. Maybe it is about numbers. Imagine you and your two best friends go on a trip – let's say to another city on a train. Among the three of you, you discuss what you want to do and agree on a plan. You make a point to ensure that if someone does not like one choice, they get first pick the next time. You share food. You make sure everyone feels involved and listened to.

But imagine taking the same trip with 300 friends. Suddenly things are much harder. How can you make sure you know what 300 people want? What if there is no agreement? What if a group of people decide they are angry and complain they are being ignored. They start threatening to leave. Some of them decide to fight to take back what they feel has been unfairly taken from them. You try to speak with them, but others yell, there is just so much noise. It feels impossible to get everyone to listen to each other.

Perhaps this is why humans go to war. Our societies get large, too large, and we can no longer listen to each other. We can't even really understand each other. If you live in a part of the country that is a desert, and I live by a river, I might struggle to understand when you complain about needing water. 'Just go get it from the river!' I might say, rolling my eyes, while you look at me like I am walking on my head.

When the USA was being established as a country the challenges of size were discussed. Did it make sense to make the USA a large country? In history empires implode. That is, they fall apart from the inside. People inside empires feel they are not being treated fairly, respected enough, and start attacking the government. Enemies realise the empire is using its resources to keep its people under control and cannot guard its borders. It is a great time to attack. War from within and from without.

In *The Federalist Letters* James Madison argued that the USA should be large so that no single faction could take over, but John Jay noted that it would be hard to create unity if the population was large and diverse. Cato[5] further argued that to keep the peace, the state should be kept small, small enough so all the people who lived there could feel they shared the same vision.[6] Looking at the USA now, with 'blue' and 'red' states in constant disagreement, some might wonder if indeed the USA is too large.[7]

More broadly, we could question if it is easier or harder to keep the peace when populations speak different languages, practice different religions, have different believes and cultures. How can peace be kept when there are different views? History has examples of diverse countries and empires who lived in peace but maintaining peace has always been a struggle. As technology spreads diverse ideas around the world, we face a new challenge: how can we keep the peace when constant new, contradictory ideas are spreading faster and faster? Maybe we need to re-think peace as something we can find in diversity, rather than in homogeneity.

Gender

You might have noticed that when we discuss Hobbes, we have focused on men. While Hobbes did mention women in his writings, he has been critiqued by Carol Pateman and others for assuming that political actors are men, and implying that women should be directed by men. The complex reality of human life which includes caring and cooperation, and the experiences of women, need to be acknowledged to create a better theory, Pateman argues. Some philosophers have wondered if this is part of where violence comes from: a focus on men as violent and competitive, which leaves out the caring side of men and also leaves out women. If women were not ignored, if women were part of the leadership of states, would our history be as violent as it has been?

The Impact of War

Maybe we should not be asking why we go to war but why we shouldn't go to war. Even if it is our instinct to fight, even if the world is set up for conflict … should we?

One of the problems with war, and with violence more generally, is that it cannot be controlled. Violence is like a fire in a dry forest. You think you are in control, but a single spark will start another fire, and another. Before you know it, you will be surrounded by flames. The very fire you started will consume you.

Philosopher Simone Weil argues that violence destroys humanity. Human beings become things: objects to count in a terrible game. War is about how many you killed versus how many your enemy killed. We forget that each of the dead was a person with dreams, with funny habits, with parents, family, and friends who treasured them.

Those who play the game, those who kill, army commanders and government leaders, also stop being humans and become monsters. J. R. R. Tolkien, author or *The Lord of the Rings,* noted that war turns men into orcs. Every time we participate in violence, we make those we hurt into things – objects to reach our goal. When we act violently, we lose our humanity. We lose the empathy and forgiveness that allows human beauty to flourish. We become beings driven only by anger, vengeance, greed.

Maybe war has been a central part of our past. But maybe it is our job to make sure it is not central to our future.

Conclusion

Thomas Hobbes had a great impact on how the west thinks about human nature: self-interested, violent, power-hungry, seeking glory. If humans are indeed like this, it is not surprising that there is war in the world. There is nothing to stop one country wanting to take other countries over. However, perhaps Hobbes was wrong. Philosophers who look at the ethics of caring, for example, note that caring is an integral part of human nature – we are innately caring creatures, not killing monsters. Other humanist philosophies, like Ubtuntu, capture this view powerfully in the saying 'I am because of who we all are', *ubuntu ngumuntu ngabantu* in Zulu.

Chapter Summary

In this chapter we have discussed Thomas Hobbes' view of human nature, exploring his 'state of nature' thought experiment by imagining explorers in outer space. We have considered whether violence is the natural and inevitable outcome of human nature and, if countries behave as self-interested humans, whether violence between countries is also inevitable. If this is the case, as realists argue, countries need to arm themselves to pre-empt attacks. Peace is achieved when a balance is found between armed countries. J. R. R. Tolkien and Simone Weil, however, argue that war destroys the humanity of those killed and those who kill. Moreover, as argued by care ethics philosophers and non-Western philosophies such as Ubuntu, the idea that humans are naturally self-interested and violent, might be mistaken. According to these philosophers, humans are caring and understand themselves in community with others. John Locke argued that the law of nature keeps humans from hurting. Locke's view supports a liberal view of international relations, where countries cooperate in the search for peace.

Pondering Points

- Do you think countries should arm themselves for peace?
- Do you think human nature might have changed across history? Have we become more or less violent?
- Do you think our education system makes us violent?

References

Bregman, Rutger. "The Real Lord of the Flies: What Happened When Six Boys Were Shipwrecked for 15 Months." *The Guardian*, May 9, 2020. www.theguardian.com/books/2020/may/09/the-real-lord-of-the-flies-what-happened-when-six-boys-were-shipwrecked-for-15-months.

Cato. In *The Complete Anti-Federalist*, edited by Herbert J. Storing, Vol. 2, 101–129. Chicago: University of Chicago Press, 1981.

Gilligan, Carol. *In a Different Voice: Psychological Theory and Women's Development*. Cambridge, MA: Harvard University Press, 1982.

Golding, William. *Lord of the Flies*. New York: Penguin Books, 2003.

Hamilton, Alexander, James Madison, and John Jay. *The Federalist: with Letters of "Brutus"*. Edited by Terence Ball. Cambridge, MA: Cambridge University Press, 2003.

Hobbes, Thomas. *Leviathan*. Edited by Richard Tuck. Cambridge, MA: Cambridge University Press, 1996.

Locke, John. *Two Treatises of Government*. Edited by Peter Laslett. Cambridge, MA: Cambridge University Press, 1988/1689.

Moffett, Mark W. "When It Comes to Waging War, Ants and Humans Have a Lot in Common." *Smithsonian Magazine*, May 14, 2019. www.smithsonianmag.com/scie nce-nature/when-it-comes-waging-war-ants-humans-have-lot-common-180972169/.

Noddings, Nel. *Caring: A Feminine Approach to Ethics and Moral Education.* 2nd ed. Berkeley: University of California Press, 2003.

Tolkien, J. R. R. *The Letters of J.R.R. Tolkien.* Edited by Humphrey Carpenter with the assistance of Christopher Tolkien. Boston: Houghton Mifflin, 2000.

Tronto, Joan C. *Moral Boundaries: A Political Argument for an Ethic of Care.* New York: Routledge, 1993.

Weil, Simone. "The Iliad, or the Poem of Force." In *Simone Weil: An Anthology*, edited by Siân Miles, 182–215. New York: Grove Press, 1986.

Who Said You Could Dance on the Table?

Questions About Rules, Contracts, Rights, and Wrongs

8   Who Should Rule?

Discussing the Perfect Government

What do King Louis XIV, Atahualpa, and Tutankhamen have in common?

They all ruled, and they all linked themselves to the sun. King Louis XIV named himself the 'Sun King'. Atahualpa, as an Inca ruler, or Sapa Inca, traced his ancestry to Manco Capac, who came from the sun. Egyptian Pharaohs like Tutankhamen linked themselves to the Sun God, Ra, arguing they guaranteed Ra's cosmic order through their rule. All these rulers saw themselves as appointed by, representing, or embodying, God.

The idea that our leaders are linked to God is still discussed, as you might notice, for example, in American, Iranian, British, and Afghan politics. And much of human history has revolved around discussions of who God appointed, if anyone, or if humans could rule themselves without God getting involved.

In our philosopher's party, there is much debate about who should be in charge to make the world a better place. Plato is clear in his position: 'Until philosophers are kings, or the kings and princes of this world have the spirit and power of philosophy, and political greatness and wisdom meet in one ... cities will never have rest from their evils' (Plato, *Republic*, Book V).

I tend to agree with Plato: only those willing to seek truth through hard years of study, and who are not driven by ambition for power and glory should lead a state ... but then I look at the philosophers we invited to our party and wonder if I would put any of them in charge of a state ...

Do As I Say, Not As I Do!

Do you like it when others tell you what to do?

I certainly don't. I can't remember any point in my life when I have thought 'Oh great! Here is someone who will boss me around and tell me what to do!'. Yet all countries have some form of government, and the role of that government

DOI: 10.4324/9781032620121-11

is, in part, to tell us what to do. You can only drive in this direction. You must not go faster than this speed. You are not allowed to eat this. You must not do this ... you must do this ... blah, blah, blah. Why do we put up with this?

You might think that without a government all would be chaos. Anarchist philosophers, such as Russian Peter Kropotkin would disagree with you. They argue that humans can cooperate and collaborate, without having anyone tell them what to do. According to anarchists, we could create a peaceful community with no one in charge of telling others what to do. Everyone would be responsible and help and contribute for everyone's benefit.

As we have seen in the chapter on war, philosopher Thomas Hobbes would strongly disagree. He would argue that without rules society would be chaotic, horrible, and deadly. Everybody would do whatever they wanted: someone might drive into my house. Someone might carry a loaded gun with them to the park.

The reason we all live under government rules, Hobbes would explain, is because we do not want to live 'like animals' without rules.[1] So, according to Hobbes, we agree to have someone tell us what to do, which means giving up some of our freedoms, for the sake of a less dangerous, more enjoyable life. You cannot, for example, drive with a blindfold. The government tells you it is illegal and will put you in jail if you do it. You lose your freedom to drive as you wish, but we all gain safety on the roads. This is a social contract – a contract between the government and the people it is taking care of.[2] The government agrees to keep you safe, and you agree to obey the rules.

In a limited way, some have argued this is also the logic of a family. Parents put in place rules (bedtime, teeth brushing, no Minecraft at 3am) and kids lose some freedoms ('Why can't I play Minecraft at 3am??!! Why can't I brush my teeth with chocolate sauce?') but in exchange kids get safety.[3]

'Hold on!', you scream. 'I did not sign any contract! I want to play Minecraft at 3am and I want to drive blindfolded!'

Seventeenth-century British philosopher John Locke looks at you and smiles, 'It is a *tacit* contract' he explains. That is, by living in your country (or in your parents' house), by using its resources – its roads, its educational system – you have entered into an implied contract. By living in your country and benefiting from the rules that keep you safe, you are agreeing to support the rules of the state. Unless you choose to leave your country, you are accepting its social contract, which means you must follow the government's rules.

Who Should Be in Charge?

If we are to have a government, who should be in charge?

Imagine you are going camping with a group of friends. You walk into the woods and find that the trail splits in two. The group needs to decide whether to follow a shorter but much steeper trail to your campsite, or a much longer path that goes around a mountain.

Maria steps out and says, 'We need a leader to guide our choice. As I have studied the map the most, and as I am a good friend to all of you, I think I should be your leader and tell you what to do'. A few in the group agree. Maria, after all, is a sensible person.

Tomas speaks up: 'No, thank you! Why should we listen to you? You might be right, but you might be wrong. We all have brains; I think we should all discuss what to do and then vote on what we want'. Rose sits by the map with her eyes closed. She speaks up: 'I think you should listen to me. God has told me she wants me to lead you'.

A discussion breaks out. Part of the group wants to follow Maria. Some think Rose has heard from the goddess. Part of the group agrees with Tomas and wants to decide what is best by voting. Part of the group wants to toss a coin. And a couple of your friends are amused by pretending to be kangaroos and have no interest in what you are discussing.

What do you think would be the best way to lead this group? Put someone in charge or have everyone vote on what path to take?

Power to the People: Democracy

The idea that all people should take part in deciding what is to be done is known as democracy and its emergence is usually traced back to ancient Athens.[4] The word *democracy* comes from the Greek *demos,* meaning the people, and *kratia*, meaning power. Democracy is rule by the people or power to the people. People power!

In ancient Athens, however, democracy only included men, born in Athens, who were not enslaved. It left out women (that is about half of the population!), children, and foreigners. People power was in fact the power of only *some* men. This has been the case throughout most of democracy's history. Very few people have had the power to be part of government, to have their ideas heard and to help choose what rules guide their lives.

Countless battles and revolutions have been fought by people demanding to be listened to, to have a voice in government. And power has slowly been extended. At first only certain men had a vote in democracies. Then certain men and women. Now, in most countries, most men and women can vote and run for office.[5] But gaining this power has been terribly hard. Suffragettes chained themselves to carts and held hunger strikes to get the right to vote in the UK. African Americans were killed in horrible ways when they demanded their right to vote in the USA. People have died for their right to be heard. And some are still not heard. Voting systems and requirements can make it hard for people to vote or make it so that some votes count more than others.

But we are assuming that we want everyone to have a voice in government. Do we? Going back to the story that started this chapter, do we want those playing kangaroos and paying no attention to tell us where to go? Is it their right to be heard even if they want to be marsupials?

Why everyone would want their voices heard is clear. Having no say in the life you lead, in the rules that govern you, is oppressive and unfair. It also makes sense why some, particularly those in power, might not want to share their power with others. After all, why would you want to give power to those who oppose you? Would you want to give the vote to those who would change things so you have less power? But, even if you wanted everyone to have a say, there are some problems with listening to all voices in a democracy, as various philosophers have pointed out. Let's look at these.

Problem 1: Should Sheep Carry Guns – Or Democracy and the Tyranny of the Masses

Imagine this. There are 20 wolves in a field. And a couple of sheep. All the animals come together to vote on what to have for dinner. This is a democracy.

The sheep are unanimous: 'Graaass, graaasss! Graaass is greeeat!' they chant.

However, the wolves are also unanimous: 'Sheeeeep! Muuuutton! Lamb!' They howl.

There are more wolves than sheep. If the government is a democracy, each wolf and each sheep get to be heard by voting. Each gets one vote. But since there are more wolves than sheep, the democracy will decide that the wolves can eat the sheep. It a clear case of 20 versus 2.

Is this fair?

Of course, this is a rather silly example as wolves are carnivorous predators and sheep are herbivorous prey … Things are a bit more complicated with humans, but a similar dynamic could happen. The majority in a country might choose to oppress a religious minority. The wishes of the majority might be to forbid the religion of the minority. In a more horrific example, the majority could decide to kill the minority.

Is this fair? Should we do what the majority of people want, even if their wish is to hurt someone? To take a different example, what if the majority of a country votes to pollute the environment, or to follow an economic policy that creates wealth in the present but will make future generations poor. Should the people have the power when they are using this power badly?

This ability of the majority to decide to act in ways that might hurt the minority, or which might go against the greatest interest of all, is what James Madison called the *tyranny of the majority*. Can democracy be set up to avoid this 'mob rule'[6]?

Problem 2: Power to the (Confused?!) People? Democracy and Information

I was just reading online about this dangerous chemical: dihydrogen monoxide. Apparently people who inhale it drown, people can choke on it, and it can seriously burn when it is hot. Sadly, this chemical is in most people's houses, often in their kitchen, because there is no regulation preventing its use. Clearly, the government should make this chemical illegal, or at least make it impossible for young children to have access to it. I am going to vote to make this chemical illegal![7]

Now, before you go to your kitchen to see if this terrible chemical is in your house let me tell you: dihydrogen monoxide is ... H_2O. Water. Water can indeed kill, but it is also necessary for life. What this example shows is that misinformation can lead to poor choices. Misinformed voters, or voters who lack enough information, can lead a democracy to wrong policies.

Technology makes it easy for misinformation to spread faster than ever before. Everyone – the informed and uninformed alike, the confused and the clever – can now easily share information for millions to see.

As technology advances, moreover, distinguishing truth from lies gets harder. Deep fakes are videos that appear to show a person saying or doing something they never did. But the video looks completely real. How can the people choose the right policies, or elect the right politicians, when we don't if what see and hear is true?[8]

Problem 3: Vote for Me, I Will Save You! Democracy and Populism

What if lots of people fell for a conspiracy theory that said the country was being taken over by killer broccolis (imagine the smell!). In the midst of the chaos a brave leader steps forward promising to rid the world of stinky brassicas (broccolis)! Fuelled by fear of all things green, masses turn out to vote and elect this leader. The voters don't care or understand how the leader will get rid of broccolis or what else he might do. They are just afraid and excited to have such a charismatic leader. He wears purple pants!

The leader promises that he *understands* the people, and that he will protect the people from immigrants who bring in smelly vegetables. The masses cheer and the leader is elected by a majority. Is this democratic? Yes. Could this happen? Yes. Is this good? Well, not unless you really dislike broccoli.[9] Once elected the 'Broccoli killer' might decide to rule for his own interests and not those of the people. But his *populist* ways managed to get him elected.

Political theorists such as Ernest Laclau and Cas Mudde have discussed how democracies can lead to populist leaders. These are leaders who are often charismatic – good speakers, funny, endearing – who present themselves as protectors of 'the people' against 'the elite' (even if they are often part of the elite themselves). They often use inflammatory language to get people to support them – making them afraid of possible dangers, or angry at apparent injustices, or inspired at what glory could be theirs in the future: 'Make our country wonderful! Beware of invading masses! Take the wealth you deserve!'.

Ancient philosopher Plato was a strong critic of democracy. He argued that democracy, would encourage leaders to follow the whims of the masses, rather than good policies, to get to power. This would result in chaos and insecurity as different, contradictory views are supported (We need to plant more trees! We need to plant only native trees! We need to plant pretty trees. We need to pull out trees! We need to sell more goods. We need to stop trading. We need nuclear power. We need to stop nuclear power ...) This is the perfect set up, argued Plato, for tyrants.[10] Tyrants rise to power by exploiting people's fears, using social divisions to advance support for their position. Once in power, tyrants rule for their benefit, not the benefit of the people.

How can democracy protect itself from populist leaders or tyrants who promise the moon, only to steal the stars?

Improving Democracy

If we want to have a democracy, we need to face the problem we have been discussing: that the majority, due to lack of information or fear, can make terrible choices. How can we make democracy better?

Liberal philosopher John Stuart Mill wondered whether some people should get more votes or whether the votes of some people should carry more weight than others. If you are more educated, for example, Mill thought you would be better able to understand what the government needs to do and, therefore, your vote should count for more. Again, going back to our initial example in this chapter – maybe those playing kangaroos could get one vote, but those who actually studied the map should get two?[11]

You might already be thinking of some problems with this approach in the real world. First, it might be the case that only rich people can afford education. Will this then mean that the rich get more votes? Also, how can we know that those more educated will truly know better? There are many people with no formal education who are thoughtful and wise, and many with multiple degrees who are selfish and unkind. Moreover, this can quickly lead us away from the ideal of democracy: everyone gets to be heard. If we give some more votes, some voices will be heard loudly, others will only be whispers.[12]

Other philosophers, such as Benjamin Barber have argued that rather than giving more votes to a few, what we need is more people participating in democracy to make a stronger democracy. The greater the discussion the less likely that a few uninformed broccoli-haters will elect a populist to power. We need voters to get involved in local organisations, local policies, voting directly rather than voting for someone to represent them. Representative democracy allows voters to elect someone and then forget all about politics until the next election. This is not what democracy is about.

Why not, for example, let younger people vote, as argued by Philosopher John Wall. Whatever choices are made by a government will, after all, affect young people much more than they will affect 80-year-olds – young people will be around for much longer! Why are we not letting those most affected by the government's choices choose the government and its rules? This is of course not about one-year-olds voting, but if tweens and teens are able to participate in sophisticated discussions, why should their voices not be heard?

What if we take the expansion of democracy further? What if we go beyond humans? So far it has been humans discussing what they want, what they need, what they want changed. And human desires and choices have caused significant damage to nature all around us. Some philosophers argue that nature should also be considered when we create governments.[13]

Conclusion

Democracy is not perfect. Ensuring everyone can be heard and vote is difficult.[14] Ensuring everyone understands what is being voted on and is interested enough to participate (remember your friends playing at being kangaroos …) is challenging. Providing education and information to prevent the majority of people from making bad and dangerous choices is difficult. But millions have fought and died for the ideal of democracy – because we would rather participate in making the rules that run our world, than have no choice over what happens to us. If we don't participate in our government, we might end up with murderous tyrants. Democracy gives us the option to change our government if it does not line up with our values. Democracy gives us the power to speak up, it is not a power we should take lightly.

However, democracy is in trouble. For democracy to be strong it needs people to participate – to make their voice heard. Democracy is not really democracy if a large part of voters fail to participate. Or if many who vote have been misled by fake news. In certain countries people's voices are being silenced. Lack of freedom to speak, to read, to gather and debate, allows misinformation to spread and poor leaders to rise. Remember, reaching democracy required the sacrifices of many – this is not something we can afford to waste.

Chapter Summary

This chapter discussed the ideal government. It departs from the question – do we need a government at all? This introduces the idea of anarchism and Kropotkin's work. If we decide we want a government that gives power to the people, democracy, we then need to understand what a democracy is, its history, and its challenges. People have fought and died to have a voice in who rules, leading to democracies expanding. But democracy is not perfect. It can lead to 'mob rule' or, as James Madison called it, the tyranny of the majority. Those voting can be misled by poor information or by populist leaders, as Plato warned and as discussed by Laclau and Mudde. To avoid such mistakes, John Stuart Mill argued for those more educated to get more votes, but this, the chapter noted, is a slippery slope toward democracy's death. Rather we need to strengthen democracy, as Barber argued, by getting people educated and involved. This is your job. John Wall argues that young people's voices should be heard – so make yours loud!

Pondering Points

- In some countries it is mandatory to participate in government. You either vote or you are fined. Do you agree with this policy? Should people have the option to not participate in a democracy?
- In ancient Athens government officials were elected by sortition – which meant any eligible citizen could be called to office if their number came up. Do you think your country should use that system now?
- Can technology change how we do democracy? What do you think of having people vote on all policies online to make democracy more direct? Or maybe having virtual meetings with government leaders?

References

Barber, Benjamin R. Strong *Democracy: Participatory Politics for a New Age*. 20th anniversary ed. Berkeley: University of California Press, 2003.

Keyssar, Alexander. *The Right to Vote: The Contested History of Democracy in the United States*. Revised ed. New York: Basic Books, 2009.

Kropotkin, Peter. "Anarchism: Its Philosophy and Ideal." In *Kropotkin's Revolutionary Pamphlets*, edited by Roger N. Baldwin, 115–144. New York: Vanguard Press, 1927.

Laclau, Ernesto. "Populism: What's in a Name?" In *Populism and the Mirror of Democracy*, edited by Francisco Panizza, 32–49. London: Verso, 2005.

Locke, John. "Second Treatise of Government." In *Two Treatises of Government,* edited by Peter Laslett, 330–333. Cambridge, MA: Cambridge University Press, 1988.

Mill, John Stuart. "Considerations on Representative Government." In *On Liberty, Utilitarianism and Other Essays*, edited by Mark Philp and Frederick Rosen, 181–393. Oxford: Oxford University Press, 2015.

Mudde, Cas. "The Populist Zeitgeist." *Government and Opposition* 39, no. 4 (2004): 541–563.

Plato. "Republic." *In* The Dialogues of Plato, Vol. 3. Translated by Benjamin Jowett. Book VIII. Oxford: Oxford University Press, 1892.

Wall, John. *Give Children the Vote: On Democratizing Democracy*. New York: Bloomsbury Academic, 2021.

Ware, Susan. *Why They Marched: Untold Stories of the Women Who Fought for the Right to Vote*. Cambridge, MA: Belknap Press of Harvard University Press, 2019.

9 How Do You Know That?

Discussing the Perfect Education

Philosophers are still discussing who should be in charge. Plato's idea of philosophers in charge has turned the discussion to what it means to learn philosophy. What is education. 'Focusing on education is right' says a kind, friendly voice. It is the voice of educational philosopher Paulo Freire. 'Education', Freire continues, 'can liberate people so they need no philosopher to guide them – they can *all* be philosophers'. This makes me think of a story.

Imagine walking down a grassy hill where you spot a cave. Pushing bravely past thorny bushes you find a tunnel that leads to a glowing emerald column. On it is a golden parchment. What does it say? Well. Hmmm. You don't know. Maybe it is a recipe for ever-lasting life. Maybe it is your aunt's secret cookie recipe (she took baking seriously!). Maybe it's a recipe for a terrible plague that could destroy the world. You don't know.

Now imagine having the knowledge to understand the parchment, or the skills to research its meaning. This is what education is: the skills to understand our world, to make sense of what seems secret and confusing.

Have you ever traveled to a country where you could not speak the local language? Think about how you felt (or imagine this experience). You cannot understand what people are saying. You might feel a bit embarrassed or stressed. Maybe you are worried that someone is going to take advantage of your ignorance. You must rely on the kindness of others.

Now, imagine if you could understand the language. You could interact with others easily, understand signs around you, be independent. This is education: freedom, understanding. Power.

DOI: 10.4324/9781032620121-12

Don't Read This Book!

Imagine a country that forbids anyone with brown eyes from reading. If a brown-eyed person is found with a book they will be punished, even killed. In fact, brown-eyed people are not allowed to learn how to read or write, and anyone found teaching them will also be punished. Imagine being a brown-eyed person. Forced to rely on others to tell you the rules. Unable to write down your ideas, your stories.

This is not an imaginary scenario.

Forced illiteracy has been a reality for many. Laws prohibiting blacks from learning to read were passed in many USA states before the Civil War. Colonial powers also forbid indigenous peoples from learning to read (for example in Latin America and Africa) or forced them to learn only the language of the colonising power, forbidding education in native languages. Even when rules changed, those previously excluded from education could only access limited, second-class education. South African comedian Trevor Noah talks about his education in apartheid South African, and notes that schools set up for non-whites limited learning to basic agricultural knowledge, giving no access to further knowledge.

This is not just an issue of skin colour or colonisation. Education for people with disabilities has been limited or non-existent. Women have been forbidden education. The Taliban still forbids girls from studying and will kill those who disobey. Why would someone want to keep others from learning? Why is education political?

Education, Knowledge, and Power

Philosopher Michel Foucault argued that knowledge and power are related. Those who have power control what others can know, and who can learn. By limiting access to knowledge, you can control others. The Protestant Reformation is an example of how this worked. Before the Reformation, the Bible was only available in Latin, which most common people could not read. Those who could read the Bible could tell others what, supposedly, God said – to disobey could mean eternal damnation, quite a scary thing! Martin Luther, one of the leaders of the Reformation, translated the Bible into German to allow common people to read it. Suddenly able to read the Bible themselves, people no longer needed the leaders to guide them to God. They started questioning the rules. They started questioning those in power.

Dolores Cacuango provides another example of how power and education are linked. Mama Dulu, as she was sometimes known, was born in 1881, in Cayambe, Ecuador. As an indigenous person, she was not allowed to access education. Indigenous people like her worked as peons for landowners in a system known as huasipungo, which tied indigenous people to the hacienda where they worked in exchange for a small plot of land where they could, theoretically, grow their own food. The system gave landowners a permanent labour force. Indigenous people often became indebted to the landowners, unable to make enough food to survive, and thus were in reality enslaved.

As a young teen Dolores ran away to avoid being forced into marriage. She walked to the city where she found employment as a domestic servant. There she learnt Spanish. She realised that if indigenous people could not read and write in Spanish, they could not understand the laws used to enslave them. She decided to set up bilingual schools where indigenous people could learn to read Spanish and Kichwa. Teaching Kichwa helped indigenous people maintain their identity and acknowledged the value of the language – challenging the elites' views that only Spanish was a language worth knowing. Dolores was arrested multiple times but continued to work to give indigenous people the education they needed to fight for their liberation and rights. This education would lay the foundation for a series of leaders who changed national laws for greater justice.

The Intrinsic and Instrumental Value of Education

Despite its importance, or perhaps because of it, education has often been a luxury of the rich. Historically, most people could not afford to pay for tutors or schools. Children were expected to work with their parents for the family to survive – they could not take time off to study. In some parts of the world, the idea of sending a girl to school is still seen as a waste: why waste time she could spend at home cleaning or tending to animals, when at the end the girl will just marry and have children. Why would she need an education?

Limiting access to education has severe consequences, not just for those denied the education, but for society at large. If your population has limited education, they are limited in the sorts of jobs they can do. If they can't read, if they can't use computers, they can only do manual work. This type of work is not very well paid. If you want your country to gain more money, therefore, you want your population to be educated. And, of course, about half of your population is female. There is, in other words, an economic incentive for governments to ensure their population is educated, including women. Education has an instrumental value – it allows people to get jobs. By providing free, or cheap education, governments can have an educated, competitive population.

This is an economic argument for education, but we could argue that education should be available not just because it could lead to a job, but because it is a human need. All humans need intellectual stimulation to feel happy and fulfilled. Education is intrinsically good – that is, it is good in itself, not because of whether it can lead to jobs or money. Education grants you the skills you need to create the life you want, to be the person you want to be. Education helps you understand yourself.

Education and Government

Paulo Freire saw education as a tool for liberation. He argued that education was not about memorising facts but rather about learning how to think. As you think about your life, what you have done, what you want, you become freer. You are no longer tied to what you have been told needs to be done, you no longer simply obey the rules. Instead you begin to understand what you want, what you need, and what needs to happen for you to get it. You might choose to stop following traditions. You might decide to break rules. This, however, might pose a problem to those in power. A government might want to limit education that leads people to break rules. A government might want to limit the discussion of ideas that might bring it down.

All governments limit access to some ideas. In countries with monarchies, for example, discussing whether monarchies should end is often prohibited. However, some governments prohibit more ideas than others. Totalitarian governments are those that try to control all ideas, and all aspects of their citizens' lives and thoughts. This would include controlling all aspects of education.

Totalitarian governments are famous for book burnings. Book burnings are a way to control what can be learnt: books that have 'wrong' ideas are burnt to make their ideas disappear. However, even countries considered democratic and free, such as the USA, have been known for banning (and burning) books (Ovenden 2020). Those who burn books argue that this is a way to protect people from harmful ideas. In particular, they argue that young people should not be exposed to every idea through education. Education should only share good, moral ideas. Do you think education should protect us from some ideas, or should all ideas be allowed in education?

You might have answered, 'Yes, I believe in freedom of thought! Bring all the ideas!' But what if a school, or a group of parents, want to teach children that cats are really overlords that should be worshipped with whisker dances? Or that the Earth is flat? Or that a certain group of people are inferior or evil? Do you think incorrect or immoral ideas should be taught?

The problem is that what ideas are wrong or immoral is not always clear. Some think that the idea that women are equal to men, for example, is wrong and immoral. Some think the idea that humans are animals is wrong and immoral. Some think that an education that does not include religion is wrong and immoral. Whose job is it to decide what is wrong or immoral and should not be taught?

Who Should Be in Charge of Education

We have already seen that governments might have vested interests that guide what ideas they support or oppose. What if parents are put in charge? They are certainly those who best know and love their children. But what if parents are mistaken? What if parents believe humans are the eggs of aliens from another universe; should they be allowed to teach this to their children? Or what if parents simply don't think their children need to learn maths or science, and choose to limit their children's education accordingly?

The Amish are a USA religious community who do not use modern technology. They do not use cars, or computers, phones, or even zippers. The Amish focus on traditional jobs and children are expected to stay within the community. Amish parents do not believe their children need advanced education to participate in community life, and that advanced education may undermine community values. Thus, Amish parents take their children out of education in middle school. The government of the state of Wisconsin, on the other hand, holds that all children should be in education until the age of 16 and argued that Amish parents could not choose to limit their children's education.

This dispute was taken to the Supreme Court which, in Wisconsin v Yoder (1972), agreed that children could not be put in compulsory education, as parents had the right to choose when and how to educate their children to protect their way of life. This meant that parents could choose to educate their children at home or in a way they saw fit to their values and culture. Do you agree with the Court's decision?

One of the challenges here is that education is both private and public. It is private because it happens at home and in your mind. It is public because it can happen in school and public places and also because it affects how you feel about others, what jobs you can get, how you act, what values you support in society. If we agree the government has a role to play to keep public spaces safe, then it has a role in education. But does this mean the government has the right to enter into your private space – your home, your thoughts – where education also happens?

Home education brings this discussion to a head. Parents opting out of a state-given education to educate their children at home might argue that a state education is insufficient, biased, or unsatisfactory, failing to give their children what they need to succeed in life. The state, on the other hand, might argue that they have the obligation to ensure their citizens are receiving an education that supports community values and prepares citizens for jobs. The state might demand to review what children are learning. Parents might demand to keep their children's education out of the state's hands. We have a war between the private and the public, the state and parents.

In the middle of this debate are children – should they be asked what they want to learn? Some philosophers, such as Ivan Illich, argued that schools should be abolished altogether to move society away from institutions that limit what can be learnt and who gets to learn. Why should we all learn the same things, at the same time, in the same way?

Without schools, without obligations, do you think all humans would choose to learn?

Plato's Allegory of the Cave – Education and Truth

Imagine you live in a cave. As far as you know, you have always lived here – tied up against a wall with a bunch of other people. Even though you cannot move much, you are quite comfortable. You are well fed, warm, and safe. As you sit there, you can see what is happening in front of you, and you spend most of your days talking about the things you see. You and the other cave-dwellers have constructed some sophisticated explanations for what you see, theories about why they exist, and predictions about the future. You are known as an expert on cave-things: Dr Cave-Things is your title.

Then one day you realise the chains that hold you to the wall have gotten loose. You pull a bit and realise you can set yourself free. Being free is terrifying because you have never left the wall before. Moving is painful and awkward. But, wow, it is also exciting! Slowly you crawl away. You crawl behind the wall that has always held you and – what! You find the most incredible thing. It is so warm and … energetic!? It is so bright that at first you just cover your eyes and want to crawl back away from it. But curiosity keeps you going. After a bit, you slowly uncover your eyes and see people putting pieces of wood into this bright thing, and it seems to eat the wood. You hear the word 'fire'. And, what? People walk between the fire and the wall that you were tied to while holding objects, and these objects make the things you have been looking at for years. Those 'things' you studied so carefully for years … you realise they are nothing but shadows. Everything you knew is nothing but the shadow of these objects.

You want to cry. But then you look to the side and see something very bright. Bravely, you decide to walk to it. You face a very steep, hard climb. You are exhausted. Every step feels like the last one you can take. You slip and scratch yourself. But curiosity keeps you going. You reach the top and realise this is a hole, a way out of the cave. The cave you have always lived in. You leave the cave and step for the first time into daylight. The pain in your eyes is incredible. You fall to the ground. Slowly, your eyes get used to the light and you look around you. The colours are so bright you do not even have words for them. And then you look up and your eyes are in pain again. It that a big ball of fire? You realise that it is the ball that light comes from. You realise just how limited your life has been. Until now you have only seen the shadows of objects representing real things.

Can you imagine what it would feel like to see the sun, to see the sky, to see trees for the first time? What would it feel like to realise that your whole life, what you thought you knew, what you thought was real, was nothing but shadows?

This is Plato's famous *Allegory of the Cave*. Plato was writing about knowledge – and noting that many people think they know, but really know nothing but shadows. He describes the process of learning as a painful journey – leaving what you are used to and comfortable with, feeling the pain of moving from a cave to sunshine, feeling the fear of walking into the unknown. Learning, according to Plato, takes great courage and determination. Most people do not want this. Most people want to happily stay in the cave, eating, drinking, and talking about shadows. And if you go and tell them there is something outside the cave, they don't want to know.

By the fact that you are reading this book, I assume you want to leave the cave. Do you agree with Plato in thinking most people do not want an education that requires them to leave the comfortable cave of shadows?

Education for the Future

Education now is not the same as education in, say, the Stone Age. A cave child would need to learn what stones are better for making weapons and how to use animal skins to make clothes. Now, you can get away without being able to tell a quartz from granite and can live your whole life without touching an animal skin … but you do need to know how to use a computer.

What do you think education for the future might entail? Should we learn foreign languages? Or will instantaneous translation make that a waste of time? Maths? Coding? Do we need to learn about the past to prepare us for the future?

What if in the future we could just sit at a computer, plug it into your brain and have information downloaded into your mind. Would that be education? Can you learn without experiences? Could you, for example, 'learn' what an orange tastes like without ever tasting one?

If we can get information 'downloaded' into our brain does this mean that we could learn without effort? This would contradict Plato's idea that climbing out of the cave is hard. But what if education is not about storing information (after all, computers are much better for this) but, rather, it is about the journey out of the cave. Maybe education is about having the determination to take each of those hard, scary steps to see things in a different light, to question whether what you believe in is true, and to keep going, even if you have to do it alone.

Conclusion

Education shapes us – how we think, what we think, how we think about ourselves. And education shapes societies – what we think is a moral way to live, what kind of jobs we can do, who we can speak with. This is why education is so strongly fought over. Governments, teachers, parents, fight over whether education should be religious, secular, censored, critical. Education can be a tool of liberation, a path out of the cave, and this is why people have sacrificed everything to access education for themselves and their families. Knowledge is power.

Chapter Summary

In this chapter we have noted that access to education has been fought over. What should be taught, who should teach, who should learn, are all controversial questions. That might be because, as argued by Paulo Freire, education can liberate people or, as noted by Michel Foucault, knowledge can be monopolised and used to oppress.

The court case between the Amish community and the state of Wisconsin provides an example of this clash over education. The chapter noted that education is always politically charged because it overlaps the public and the private. Education affects how a society works, and it takes place in homes, inside our minds, in areas that we might not want any government intervention. We discussed Plato's Allegory of the Cave as an allegory on education. And we finished by considering what education in the future might be like – will we get our education via cloud transfers into our brain in the future?

Pondering Points

- Do you think education can change human nature, or do you think some people are smarter, nicer, or more violent than others and education cannot affect this?
- Do you think a certain amount of education – or certain subjects like maths – should be mandatory for all the citizens of a country (or even of the world)?
- I once had a student who told me he studied hard so his parents would not be punished by the government. Do you think parents should be responsible for the education of their children?

References

BBC News. "Oklahoma Orders Schools to Teach Bible 'Immediately'." *BBC News*, June 28, 2024. www.bbc.co.uk/news/articles/cjk35vv2ryjo.

Brown, Kimberley. "In the Footsteps of Ecuador's 'Mama Warrior'." *Atlas Obscura*, March 31, 2022. www.atlasobscura.com/articles/dolores-cacuango-ecuador-mama-warrior.

Foucault, Michel. *Power/Knowledge: Selected Interviews and Other Writings, 1972–1977*. Edited by Colin Gordon. Translated by Colin Gordon, Leo Marshall, John Mepham, and Kate Soper. New York: Pantheon Books, 1980.

Freire, Paulo. *Pedagogy of the Oppressed: 30th Anniversary Edition*. New York: Bloomsbury Publishing USA, 2014.

Illich, Ivan. *Deschooling Society*. New York: Harper & Row, 1971.

Noah, Trevor. *Born A Crime*. London, England: John Murray, 2017.

Ovenden, Richard. *Burning the Books*. Cambridge and London, England: Harvard University Press, 2020. https://doi.org/10.4159/9780674249509.

Span, C. M. "Learning in Spite of Opposition: African Americans and their History of Educational Exclusion in Antebellum America." *Counterpoints* 131 (2005): 26–53. www.jstor.org/stable/42977282.

U.S. Reports: Wisconsin v. Yoder, 406 U.S. 205 (1971). [Periodical] Retrieved from the Library of Congress. www.loc.gov/item/usrep406205/.

Wodon, Q., C. Montenegro, H. Nguyen, and A. Onagoruwa. *Missed Opportunities: The High Cost of Not Educating Girls. The Cost of Not Educating Girls Notes Series.* Washington, DC: The World Bank, 2018.

Yousafzai, Malala, and Christina Lamb. *I Am Malala: The Girl Who Stood Up for Education and Was Shot by the Taliban.* New York: Little, Brown and Company, 2013.

10 Who Owns What?

Discussing Ownership and Reparations

The philosopher's party continues. Socrates has taken the idea of a party to heart and is attempting the running man with Slavoj Žižek … but other philosophers are seriously discussing the origin of our problems. How did we get to this place, where some don't have enough to survive and wars spread like cancer?

Jean Jacques Rousseau stands up and, banging his fist on the table, shouts: 'I have said it before and I will say it again "The first person who built a fence around some land and said 'This is mine,' and found people silly enough to believe him, was the true founder of civil society. What crimes, wars, murders, what miseries and horrors would we have avoided, had someone pulled up the fence and cried out to his fellowmen, 'Do not listen to this imposter'!". Now we have great inequalities! We must return to a more natural state!'[1]

'Of course, in communism everyone will share ownership', started Marx.

Nozick quietly goes up to Marx and takes a big bite out of his cake.

'Excuse me, what do you think you are doing?' protested Marx pulling on his beard.

'Well, I thought we could start now, owning cake in common', laughed Nozick running away from Marx.

Nozick is just causing trouble. After some giggles he argues that 'Individual rights are key – if a person justly acquires wealth, then it would not be fair to take that away from them to give to others. We would end up with a large government constantly taking and giving – destroying our rights'.

'I am uncertain why we need to have this conversation at all', jumps in Alberto Acosta, 'Why do we need to spend our energy discussing what to own. Can't we move away from this greed to own all things, even own people, own nature?'

DOI: 10.4324/9781032620121-13

When Does Something Become Yours?

You are walking into a forest and come across an apple tree. Delicious, crunchy, sweet apples. You pick a couple of the apples that have fallen on the floor and bite into them with delight.

Another person walks up to the tree, close behind you. They look at you then at the tree and smile. An apple would be a perfect snack for their walk.

As they approach the tree you pick up a stick 'What are you doing?', you yell, 'This is my tree'. They look confused.

'Hey, this is a public tree, in a public forest, it is not yours! It belongs to no one, and anyone can take an apple!'

'No! I found the tree. I identified the tree. I picked up the apples. Now you come here, and want to benefit from my work and take my apples? Forget it!'.[2]

Are you being reasonable here?

Well, to decide that we need to take a step back and decide what makes something yours, or mine, or theirs. How do we establish ownership?

This is a huge question. I am sure you can think of times when you have thought about this. You go to the kitchen and there is one slice of cake left. Who does it belong to? The oldest person in the house? Whoever saw it first? Whoever had less food? The person who made or bought the cake? Or, whoever ate all their vegetables?

Arguments about ownership do not stay within families. Arguments about ownership have driven history. When Cristopher Columbus landed on what became known as the Americas, he was soon followed by other Europeans who 'claimed' ownership of the land for Spain, for Portugal, for Britain, for France … . What right did these European countries have to come to land where other people already lived and claim ownership?

A few arguments were given. Some invoked god and said it was god's will for Europeans to take the land. Of course the indigenous inhabitants of the Americas had their own gods who, presumably, disagreed with this argument. Others argued that because the native inhabitants had not built what Europeans considered proper settlements, they had not put in the work necessary to be considered owners of the land they lived on. So, Europeans could take the lands, use them 'properly' and own them.[3]

We could take this debate to a higher point – should anything be owned at all? In Western cultures, there has been a tradition to think of nature as something we can own. We own land. We own animals. We even own water. But does it make sense, is it correct? Water is basic for survival – should some humans own it and keep others from having what they need to live? And what about owning living things – is it ethical to own a being that can think and feel?

Moreover, as we better understand how nature is interconnected, how everything is global, how does it make sense to own a river when that same water will flow into the ocean, be used by others, and then rain onto other lands ... how can we 'own' water?

How would the world be different if we thought about nature, about our planet, as something we all *belong* to, rather than something a few of us can *own*?

Reparations

One of the debates that comes up with discussions on ownership is what should be done about things that were taken from others. Things that were stolen. When Europeans took over the land where indigenous people lived, they did not pay for it. Now we look back on these events and realise they were unjust. The question then is, should we do something about these wrongs that were committed in the past?
Choose your answer:

Yes – there should be reparation for land and property that were taken from indigenous peoples.
No – there should not be reparations for land and property that were taken from indigenous peoples.

When considering your answer to the question, have you thought about who would pay and whom would be paid? This is one of the difficulties with addressing injustices from the past. If your neighbour comes over and takes your car, it is pretty straightforward that your neighbour should pay you back for the car they took. However, if it was your neighbour's great-great-great grandmother who took your great-great-great-granduncle's donkey, are your neighbours responsible for what their ancestors did? And are you the rightful recipient for the reparations? After all, you are only one of many descendants.

So far, we have spoken about taking over land and belongings. However, things get much more difficult, and painful, when we talk about taking people. Slavery is one of the cruellest things humans have done. Slavery is taking another person, their family, and treating them as things. Buying and selling them. Abusing and killing them. In other words *dehumanising* them. The transatlantic slave trade, where millions of people from Africa were trapped, kidnapped, enslaved, and abused to develop the wealth of European empires and the USA, is one of the greatest atrocities humanity has committed.

Clearly, taking people is a much greater crime than taking property or land. How can reparations be made for lives destroyed, for families broken, for people tortured and killed?

We know that slavery not only impacted those who suffered through it but also their descendants in multiple ways. In biology we know now that stress affects the health of a person's descendants. Slavery also meant that for generations people worked without being able to accumulate any wealth from their work. Most often they were also prohibited from accessing education. Thus, when those enslaved finally gained their freedom, they found themselves without any wealth, with limited education, with no resources, and with great trauma. Survivors and descendants of slavery had to overcome great inequalities to subsist and advance. The inequalities did not end with slavery, as racism and prejudices have limited opportunities for descendants of enslaved people up to the present day.

However, if we talk about reparations for those who were taken as slaves we come to a very difficult question. How much is a person worth? How much should the descendants of those who were enslaved be paid? Surely, it is impossible to put a price on a human life. We can quantify, somewhat, how much work they might have done. But there is no amount of money I would sell my family for. How, then, can we even enter this discussion?

You might be surprised to find out that instead of paying reparations to those who were enslaved and their descendants, reparations have been paid to those who owned slaves. As part of the negotiations to make slavery illegal in the UK, for example, the government agreed to pay slave owners for the slaves they would lose. This debt was paid into the twenty-first century.[4] On the other hand, reparations for those who suffered from slavery and colonisation – that is the taking over of land by a conquering state and the destruction of existing culture and institutions – is something that is still being debated and has yet to be resolved.

Common Ownership and Marxism

Karl Marx was a philosopher and economist who was also interested in the idea of ownership. He looked at ownership historically and noted that in most societies few people owned what he called the means of production: the machines and land you need to make or grow things to sell. Meanwhile, most people owned nothing more than their body and their capacity to work.

In the past the king owned the kingdom[5] – which meant everything. His Lords managed parts of the kingdom. And the great majority of the people, the peasants, owned nothing but their own bodies. They worked to survive and pay the Lords, who paid the King. This was a feudal system. Peasants rose up against the unfair system and sought to overthrow kings and lords and gain power.

Technology advanced and we moved to a new stage in history where a few people, or the bourgeoisie, own the factories, and most people, the proletariat, own only their bodies. This is the capitalist system. The proletariat work long hours just to afford enough to survive. However hard they work, workers can never achieve more than survival. Meanwhile, according to Marx, the bourgeoisie grow richer, benefiting from the labour of the proletariat.

Just as once peasants fought against the king owning all things, labourers would someday fight for a fairer world, where their labour would not just go to make the rich richer. All history, Marx argued, is the history of these *class* struggles. History is the fight between the haves and the have nots. Every revolution, every struggle, has been about changing things so that not just one, or not just a few, own all the wealth while the rest work to barely survive.

Marx argued that as humanity evolved we would achieve a fairer distribution of resources. Eventually, according to Marx, we would reach an ideal[6] situation called *communism*. In communism everyone would jointly own the means of production (that is we would all own the factories, and the land, and the resources to produce things). There would be no haves and have nots. In communism everyone would give as they were able, and receive as much as they needed. This is what Marx meant when he said 'From everyone according to their ability, to everyone according to their needs'.[7]

What do you think of Marx's ideal?

As you probably know communism and Marxism are very controversial.[8] The Cold War was fought, in part, over whether countries should seek communism or capitalism. Here, however, we should separate the idea from the practice. Marx saw communism as an ideal humans would eventually arrive at. It is not what Lenin, Mao, or Stalin, the Soviet Union, China, or Cuba, and so many others achieved by taking away people's liberties and having the state tell everyone what to produce. In fact, according to Marx, in communism there would be no state, no government to tell us what to do as everyone would do what is needed. A country with a big dictatorial state has very little to do with the *ideal* of communism.

Moving away from these failed attempts at communism, do you think the ideal is possible? Think about what you know about human nature (whether you agree with Hobbes, or Locke, or Noddings, as discussed in the first section of this book): do you think humans could jointly own all things and work for the common good without a government to dictate what needs to happen, without individual selfishness getting in the way?

In contrast to communism, capitalism is based on private ownership of the means of production and competition. This system allows, in theory, the most courageous, creative, and intelligent people to succeed and make a profit. The focus is on allowing individuals to profit from their work. Capitalism does not focus on the unequal ownership of the means of production and how hard it is for those who own nothing to become owners. Capitalists might argue that it is hard, but not impossible, and hard work pays off. Do you agree?

What Does the State Own?

Without focusing on whether we think the ideal of communism should be sought, we can consider whether a state, or the government of a country, should ever have the right to take from some to give to others.

In most countries the state takes away from some to give to others. This is what taxes are. In most countries part of the money you make[9] is taken back by the government. The government then spends some of this money on services we all use, to help those in need, and to pay itself.[10]

Fire departments are an example of services we all benefit from. If your house goes on fire, you can rely on the fire department to try to save you, your belongings, and your neighbourhood. However, most of us will, hopefully, never use the fire department. Why should we all, therefore, pay for it?

I am personally extremely careful and never leave the oven on, turn off all electricity, put out all fires, and test my appliances every year. So why should my money be spent on something I will most likely never use? If someone is irresponsible enough to start a fire surely they should pay for it.[11] In a similar way, if someone is not working, why should my money be used to feed them! Or if someone chooses to smoke, surely they should be responsible for doctor's bills if they get lung cancer! Do you agree?

There are a couple of issues to consider regarding the morality of taxes. First, we could ask ourselves, do we have a moral obligation to help those in need? If someone's house is burning, or if they are hungry and need food, should we help out of empathy or compassion? Or should we only help those who deserve help? Would you stand by and let your neighbour's house burn down to teach them a lesson because they tried to dry their socks in the oven?

Second, we might notice that your laundry-in-the-oven neighbour's fire will not stay in their house. Fire does not respect reasons or personal boundaries. It will jump to your house. Problems affect not just an individual but a community. Is helping our neighbours, therefore, also a way to help ourselves?

Of course, you might think there is a responsibility to help others, but the government has nothing to do with this – if you want to help your neighbour you can go on and help them. You do not need to give money to the state and then trust the state to help. The government might be ineffective and waste the money painting light poles different colours every month. The state might be corrupt and misuse the money. The state might give money to causes you disagree with. Libertarian thinkers, such as Robert Nozick, would argue that we need to make sure the government stays as small as possible. Larger governments are not only wasteful, but they also start to take away our rights and freedom as they tell us what to do and take our hard earned money. We should do what we think is best and not allow the state to take our property or limit our choices by putting our money in areas we would not choose to spend it. Perhaps it makes sense, however, to have the state set up fire departments, rather than try to set up a committee with your neighbours to agree who needs to fill emergency buckets each week?

Do You Believe in Invisible Hands?

One of the big debates in economics and politics is whether the state should be involved in economic processes at all. Would things work better if the government told us what to produce, what to sell, who to give money to and when ... or should we let everyone choose what to do and when to do it?

Moral philosopher Adam Smith considered this. He noted, for example, that a baker does not make bread because he wants to feed others. A florist does not sell bouquets because he wants to make houses nice. Florists and bakers might, of course, also have nice intentions and be happy that people are fed and have pretty flowers. But they sell their work to make money. It is their interest that drives them to make what other people want – because they can sell it and make money from this. And this self-interest works very effectively to get people to make what others want and need.

If everyone follows their own interest, everyone will try to produce what others want (that is how to make money!) and all that is needed will be produced without the government having to get involved. That is, the *invisible hand of the market* will make sure that everything we need is made and that it is made at the best possible price. If a florist tries to sell their flowers for a million dollars, they are unlikely to have many customers (except maybe for a celebrity with more money than sense). The florist would then be forced to lower their price or sit on piles of wilting and decomposing flowers.[12]

It is important to note, however, that Adam Smith never thought that the markets should be allowed to decide everything. For example, if you decided that selling drugs would make some good money, Adam Smith did not think 'go forth and make others addicts!' He thought society has a responsibility to protect the vulnerable, which means limiting or forbidding some market transactions. This links us back to slavery. If we allow a complete free market – this would include buying and selling humans – even human parts! But if we have a sense of ethics, we will realise that no amount of money makes it ok to buy and sell people.

Externalities are another reason why a government might want to get involved in what is sold/bought in markets. Externalities are costs that are not captured in the price of something. Let's go back to fire departments. Remember your laundry-in-the-oven neighbour (don't accept any dinner invites to their house!), the fire in their house is not just his problem. It is all of the neighbours' problem. Even if your house does not burn down, you will be affected by your neighbour's smoke. People with asthma might have a serious health crisis. These are negative externalities. By stopping the fire, the government stops you and others from being hurt.

Smoking is a much clearer example. If you choose to pretend to be a human chimney and smoke or vape (don't do it!), you might think 'Well, this is my choice, I pay for the cigarettes!'. The problem is that the smoke you produce does not stay just on your head, it goes out and might make kids playing around you, or your elderly neighbours, sick. The government might choose to discourage you from smoking through taxes or laws not because it is bad for you, but because of how it hurts those who do not choose to smoke but are affected by your choices.

There are also positive externalities: if you read this book, and you discuss the ideas in the book with friends, you are spreading information, critical thinking, and maybe some humour (at least I laugh at my jokes) to friends who have not paid for the book (of course, go ahead and encourage them to buy it ☺).

Conclusion

The main point of this chapter is that economic discussions, such as what we own, what we buy, what we sell, cannot be separated from moral philosophy. Each action we take is based on views about what/who we are responsible for, what gives us the right to own something, and what can be owned. I hope we all agree that it is immoral to own humans. However, many might still think that it makes sense to own animals, or own plants … But some philosophers, particularly those who think outside the Western mind frame, ask us to question whether any living thing can be owned. Can we ever own the Earth, or are we part of it, owned by it rather than owning it. This will be discussed further, and we will meet Acosta again, in the next section of this book.

Chapter Summary

In this chapter we have discussed the idea of ownership – noting that Rousseau saw this as the beginning of modern society and much of its troubles. We have considered how we come to own things – and whether ownership makes sense. The rights to ownership, and what should be done to repair ownership that was unfair, have been discussed with reference to colonialism and slavery. There are no simple solutions given. Similarly, there are no simple solutions when discussing what the role of government should be when it comes to ownership and distribution of resources. Nozick argues for a minimal state, to maximise individuals' freedom. Adam Smith spoke of the 'invisible hand of the market' to organise the provision of all necessary goods at an ideal price, but Smith also noted that the state needed to ensure morality was protected. Marx saw human history as a struggle between those who have and those who lack, arguing that communism is an ideal we would eventually reach. Can ideals be reached in economics? Communism and capitalism are both ideals, neither of which has led to human happiness.

Pondering Points

- If we could restart human civilisation so that there were no inequalities, do you think inequalities would creep up? Why?
- Can universal basic income solve Marx's prediction that have-nots will, eventually, enter into conflict with those who have?
- Should there be a limit on personal wealth? If one person owned 99% of the world's wealth, would that be a problem?

References

Abulafia, David. *The Discovery of Mankind: Atlantic Encounters in the Age of Columbus.* New Haven: Yale University Press, 2008.

Acosta, Alberto. "The Rights of Nature: A Philosophical and Legal Battle Between the Domination of Nature and Living in Harmony with Nature." In *The Climate Crisis: South African and Global Democratic Eco-Socialist Alternatives*, edited by Vishwas Satgar, 237–257. Johannesburg: Wits University Press, 2018.

Berlin, Ira. *Generations of Captivity: A History of African-American Slaves.* Cambridge, MA: Harvard University Press, 2003.

Bowers, Mallory and Rachel Yehuda. 'Intergenerational Transmission of Stress in Humans'. *Neuropsychopharmacol* 41 (2016): 232–244. https://doi.org/10.1038/npp.2015.247

Boxill, Bernard R. "A Lockean Argument for Black Reparations." *The Journal of Ethics* 7, no. 1 (2003): 63–91.

Coates, Ta-Nehisi. "The Case for Reparations." *The Atlantic*, June 2014.

Draper, Nicholas. *The Price of Emancipation: Slave-Ownership, Compensation and British Society at the End of Slavery.* Cambridge, MA: Cambridge University Press, 2010.

Locke, John. "Second Treatise of Government." In *Two Treatises of Government*, edited by Peter Laslett. Cambridge, MA: Cambridge University Press, 1988.

Marx, Karl. "Critique of the Gotha Program." In *The Marx-Engels Reader*, edited by Robert C. Tucker, 525–541. New York: W. W. Norton & Company, 1978.

Marx, Karl, and Friedrich Engels. *The Communist Manifesto.* Translated by Samuel Moore. London: Penguin Books, 2002.

Nozick, Robert. *Anarchy, State, and Utopia.* New York: Basic Books, 1974.

Pagden, Anthony. *Lords of All the World: Ideologies of Empire in Spain, Britain and France c.1500–c.1800.* New Haven: Yale University Press, 1995.

Rousseau, Jean-Jacques. "A Discourse on the Origin of Inequality." In *The Social Contract and Discourses*, translated by G. D. H. Cole, 27–113. London: J.M. Dent and Sons, 1913.

Smith, Adam. *An Inquiry into the Nature and Causes of the Wealth of Nations.* Edited by Edwin Cannan. Chicago: University of Chicago Press, 1976.

Smith, Adam. *The Theory of Moral Sentiments*. Edited by D. D. Raphael and A. L. Macfie. Indianapolis: Liberty Fund, 1982.

Veblen, Thorstein. *The Theory of the Leisure Class*. Oxford World's Classics. Oxford: Oxford University Press, 2007.

Wilkerson, Isabel. *The Warmth of Other Suns: The Epic Story of America's Great Migration*. New York: Random House, 2010.

Williams, Robert A. Jr. *The American Indian in Western Legal Thought: The Discourses of Conquest*. New York: Oxford University Press, 1990.

Yao, Youli, Alexandra M. Robinson, Fabiola R. Zucchi, Jerry C. Robbins, Olena Babenko, Olga Kovalchuk, Igor Kovalchuk, David M. Olson, and Gerlinde A. S. Metz. "Ancestral Exposure to Stress Epigenetically Programs Preterm Birth Risk and Adverse Maternal and Newborn Outcomes." *BMC Medicine* 12, no. 121 (2014). https://doi.org/10.1186/s12916-014-0121-6.

11 Should Humans Be Like Geese?

Discussing Migration and Citizenship

'If we want to make the world a better place', says philosopher Kwame Anthony Appiah, 'this should be for all people, wherever they live. We are surely responsible to improve the wellbeing of all, not just those who share our nationality. After all we are all humans.'

'Indeed', intervenes Joseph Carens, 'to improve the world we cannot be limited by the borders of countries. People should be able to move to where they can do better. They should be able to move freely. Having our chances determined by the luck of where we are born, what nationality we are given, is unfair. Humans should be able to move around the world. Freedom of movement is surely a human right.'

Many philosophers tell us about their experiences as immigrants and refugees. Aristotle tells everyone how he fled Athens, worried that he might be killed for his views as Socrates was. Descartes also left his home country seeking intellectual freedom. Arendt tell us how she escaped Germany and had no citizenship once the Nazis took it away. She traveled as a refugee, seeking a new place to feel safe in, to call home.

It seems like many philosophers have experienced migration. Some of their ideas, like Arendt's, were deeply shaped by being migrants or refugees. I wonder how many of these philosophers would not have been able to think, write, or speak if they had not been able to emigrate? Would our world be better if we made migration something everyone could do?

You and a couple of friends decided you have been reading enough philosophy – you need a break! You decide to go traveling and visit all the countries that have imaginary national animals.[1] You are about to start purchasing tickets when you realise you need a visa, or permit, to enter some of these countries. No problem at all, you whip out your Japanese passport and all is well. Japan has one of the most 'powerful' passports, meaning it allows you to travel to most countries

DOI: 10.4324/9781032620121-14

in the world with no need to get a visa, or with very easy to get visas – just fill in a form, pay a small fee, and you are in! But two of your friends have very 'weak' passports. Obtaining a visa for them requires putting together a pile of documents that is bigger than a book, spending hundreds if not thousands of dollars, and waiting for months to hear if they will be allowed to travel.

This seems unfair to you. Surely, everyone who wants to travel should be able to. Why is traveling so easy for you, and so hard for your friends? For you traveling is pretty much getting on a plane and crossing the skies, while for your friends traveling is like climbing one great wall after the next.

Walls and Borders

The walls are not only metaphorical. At times countries have erected great walls to stop individuals from entering or leaving. You might have heard about some of the most controversial walls. During the Cold War a metaphorical 'Iron Wall' divided the world between the area led by the USA and the area led by the USSR. A physical wall, however, was also built in Berlin, dividing the side controlled by the USA from the side controlled by the USSR. As the Soviet government grew more oppressive and the Soviet economy worsened, people wanted to cross the border and immigrate to the West. The wall became increasingly guarded. A concrete wall, razor wires, soldiers patrolling, flood lights, watch towers. Later microphones were put in the ground to detect any attempts to tunnel under the wall.

Despite all these security measures, however, people were relentless in seeking to cross the border. The desire for freedom, for opportunity, for adventure, was more important to people than the danger of crossing the wall. Many died attempting to cross. Some made it across in incredible ways. Cars had the sponge in their seats carved out so that humans could hide inside the seats. A family sewed a hot air balloon and floated across the border.

In 1989 the Berlin Wall was brought down with cheers of jubilation heard around the world. Yet while one wall fell, there are others that stand and grow, separate people, and limit people's choices. The wall between Mexico and the United States, the wall separating Israel and Palestine are just two of the most infamous.

Should these walls stand?

Open Borders – Safety, Economics, and History

Walls are, of course, only physical manifestations of the borders between countries. Even when there are no physical walls, you need permission to cross borders between countries.

Would you advocate for the abolishing of all borders, the end of all walls? Should people be free to move across the world?

Some, such as philosopher Joseph Carens, argue that freedom of movement is a human right. Humans, after all, have been moving around since we came into existence. Humans, like other animals, migrate looking for better opportunities. Think of geese, who move from the cold to the warmth and back to give their offspring the best chance to survive. Would it be reasonable to create a boundary and stop geese from migrating, to keep them in one place, or away from another? If we did, geese would either not survive or have to adapt extensively. Yet, this is what we do to humans. We tell them they need to stay in a place, even if they are unsafe, or even if there is not enough food for them there.

Of course, if we got rid of borders, we would be getting rid of countries. Without borders there would be no countries. We could consider cosmopolitanism – the view that we are all 'citizens of the world' – and move away from limitations imposed by nation-states. But in a world without state governments, how would order be set?

Borders are in fact a matter of order and protection. Think of your house. Imagine if you had no door. Anyone could come in and out of your house as they wished. It might be wonderful for your friends to come and visit, for your family to drop in and bring gifts or food whenever they wanted. But what if there is someone you do not like? Someone who might hurt you – and you do not have a door to close and keep them out! This is one argument used to support borders. Countries need to keep themselves safe from enemies, and borders help them do this. Checking who comes in and who leaves, helps a country, for example, avoid terrorists.

Yet is safety from a possible enemy, worth limiting the freedoms of thousands, of millions of people?

There is also an economic argument to be discussed here. Borders do not only keep possible dangers out, they also keep possible labourers out. The USA and Europe have seen the impact of decreasing migrant workers – for example fruit left to rot on the branches. Migrants work long, hard hours in the sun, at times exposed to dangerous pesticides, for little pay. Foreign workers can come into a country to do the work locals do not want to do.

Open borders allow more workers to come into the country, workers who are willing to work hard, for less pay. However, this also means that foreign workers can come into the country and compete with the national workers. They can be more prepared, and ready to work harder, for less money, than locals. They can take jobs away from the locals, they can push the price of labour down. Are the economic benefits worth the costs?

Golden Visas

For some, borders don't really exist. If you have enough money, entry into many countries can be bought. These paid-for-visas have been called golden visas – a golden ticket into almost any country. If you have enough money, you can buy the right to enter, or even buy citizenship, to a number of safe, economically well-off countries – including the USA, Canada, and Grenada.

To some this makes sense – for every new golden visa a country gains a new wealthy resident/citizen who might start new businesses, buy new houses ... But, you might ask, shouldn't being part of a country be about more than having the money to pay for a golden visa? If you just pay to enter a country, knowing you can pay to go live someplace else tomorrow, would you feel any sense of loyalty, or belonging? If you don't feel part of a community, what interest would you have in helping it prosper?

Blood or Land

Think about where you live now. How did you come to be there? How did you become a citizen of your state? It is likely that you gained citizenship to your country in one of two ways: *jus sanguinis* or *jus soli*.

Jus sanguinis means gaining citizenship by the right of the blood: citizenship is passed through the blood of your family – whether this is your mother, your father, both, or another ancestor like a grandfather, depends on the country. Citizenship, this view holds, is inherited, it is part of your family. Whether you are born here or on the Moon, you will still belong to the same nation as your parent, you are from your parent's blood and, therefore, from their nation.

Jus solis is the opposite. It means gaining citizenship by the rule of the land. This means that regardless of who your family is or where they are from, if you are born on this land, then this land will give you citizenship. If your parents are on a weekend holiday to Tuvalu, for example, and you are born there, even if your parents had never been there before and have no plans to return, you have the right to be a citizen of Tuvalu.

Why might a country want citizenship to be passed through the bloodline of their citizens, even if they are outside the country's borders? And why might a country want to grant citizenship to people born on its land, even if their parents are from another place?

Who a state grants citizenship to is part of how a state builds itself – who is part of its community and who is not. When the USA became a country people who had been brought to the Americas as slaves from Africa were not citizens of the state. This is not surprising as they were not considered people but property. When slavery was abolished in the USA, African-Americans were left in a state of limbo: they were not citizens of any state. Citizenship by blood was impossible: many did not know who their family was, since children were often taken from their mothers and sold separately. Most did not know where in Africa their ancestors had been abducted from. The only way to grant those who had been enslaved citizenship was to create citizenship *jus solis*. Thus, the Constitution of the United States was amended to grant citizenship to those born in the USA even if their parents had been born in a different land – which was the case for all those who had been enslaved.

However, the idea of citizenship by land has become controversial in the USA. Donald Trump argued that this type of citizenship allows illegal immigrants who have children in the USA a way to claim the right to stay – through their American citizen children. Thus, citizenship by *jus solis* has become a controversial topic in the USA. A question to consider is to what extent children should be punished by the actions of their parents: if their parents are not in a country legally, does this mean the children should be denied citizenship, denied the opportunity to integrate, even if they *feel* American. These children might become stateless if they do not qualify for citizenship in other countries. Their children might also be left without citizenship. Moreover, taking away the right of citizenship by land erases part of the history of the USA, it erases the reason why the 14th Amendment was created.

The debate about citizenship in the USA brings up larger questions about what belonging means. During the Great Depression, to increase access to work for white-Americans moving West to escape the dust bowl that was destroying farm lands, the US border patrol, with the support of local governments, launched campaigns to detain those assumed to be Mexican, including up to 1 million[2] USA-born citizens, and forced these people on transports headed to Mexico.[3] During WWII, the USA rounded up American citizens of Japanese ancestry and forced them into internment camps, ironically claiming this was done for the safety of American citizens.

What does it mean to be a citizen, to feel you belong to a nation, if this nation can turn against you unexpectedly? This is not, sadly, something unique to the USA.

After WWII, the UK invited Caribbean people, who were at the time UK subjects, to migrate to the UK to help rebuild the economy and increase the labour force. Later, however, many of these people – who had lived more than half a century in the UK, who considered the UK their home, and many of whom had been born in the UK – were detained and threatened with deportation when they could not prove their right to be in the UK. They struggled to prove their right to be in the UK because the state had failed to provide them with the right documents and had also lost their immigration records. The unfair treatment of this Windrush Generation (named after one of the vessels that transported them to the UK), came to light in the early twenty-first century.

It would be naïve to not point to skin colour and racism in the examples listed above. Those sent away, those put away, those questioned, were not random, they were people assumed to not 'belong' in a state because of their skin colour, their name, their ancestry.

Losing Your Citizenship

Having no citizenship, being kicked out of the country where you think you belong, and finding yourself wondering where you can go, and where you can feel safe, is terrifying.

Philosopher Hannah Arendt experienced losing her citizenship and reflected on her experiences in her political philosophy. Arendt was born to a Jewish family in Germany. The Nazi government began taking away the citizenship of Jews in 1935 (and of others they saw as enemies of the state, such as communists). Arendt, like other Jews, found that without citizenship she could no longer use the laws of the state to protect her. The law protected citizens, not people with no nationality. Arendt fled Germany to avoid being killed. She lived for a time in France and then fled to the USA.

Arendt realised that once Germany had taken away her citizenship, she, as stateless person, had no rights. Her right to live, to safety, to property, any right we might think humans should have, were protected, enforced, by the state. If the state did not recognise her, she had no rights. She needed citizenship to have rights.

But if the state can take away your citizenship at will, where does this leave you? How can societies exist if we can have no sense of trust in the state that upholds our rights?[4]

Arendt's experiences are similar to those of millions of people who are displaced from their homes due to war and violence. If they are unable to prove where they come from – and many people in the world have no formal documents to prove their citizenship or identity – if they are born in the middle of a war, in another country while fleeing, or in a refugee camp, or if their parents are killed in a war, and the children end up as refugees – how can they prove where they came from, how can they prove what state they belong to? Without this belonging, who is there to fight for their rights? What rights do they have if there is no state to support them?

Citizenship, Immigrants and the Social Contract

One of the reasons immigration can be controversial is because it questions the idea of a social contract. That is the idea that the state gives the people protection in exchange for their support and obedience. Immigrants can be seen as changing or expanding the contract. Is the state responsible to immigrants? Are immigrants responsible in the same way as citizens? Do they have to prove their allegiance to the contract? What if they are illegal immigrants, does this mean the state owes them nothing ... will they be killed, abused? Or is there a basic protection the state should give even to those who break its laws and come in illegally?

Is citizenship a contract that individuals or the state can end at will? Can I, for example, decide that I disagree with what my government is doing and renounce my citizenship? And, if I do this, can I ever get this citizenship back? Clearly, if one can opt in and out of a country at will, the value of the contract starts to diminish. Yet those able to obtain golden visas are able to do this with little criticism. Non-golden-visa migrants are possibly more aware of the contract a state requires than those who have always lived in a country, since they are making an explicit choice to join the contract.

Conclusion

The idea of cosmopolitanism has a long history. Stoic philosophers in Ancient Greece argued for the idea of common humanity. Kwame Anthony Appiah argues that we can think of ourselves as global citizens while also respecting our local identities. As the world becomes more interconnected with faster travel and digital connections, perhaps our notion of citizenship needs to change. There are millions of people around the world who identify with a state they don't live in, a state perhaps their parents or even grandparents were born in – these are known as the *diaspora*. Perhaps, therefore, we need to rethink what citizenship is: perhaps we can belong to more than one place, perhaps we can eventually see all of us as belonging to planet Earth as much as to any one state.

Chapter Summary

This chapter has considered the logic and ethics of citizenship and immigration. We started by considering whether countries should have borders or whether people should be able to freely move around the planet, as argued by Carens. Cosmopolitanism, the idea of being a citizen of the world, supported by philosophers such as Kwame Anthony Appiah, might allow such movement. However, Hannah Arendt, who suffered as a refugee and immigrant herself, argues that citizenship in a state is key, as it is states that administer and protect individual's rights. The chapter further discussed whether citizenship should be based on one's ancestry, one's place of birth, or one's ability to pay an immigration fee. Does it matter whether one feels a sense of belonging to a state? And, further, under what conditions should a state, if ever, remove an individual's citizenship? These two questions highlight the social contract on which citizenship and immigration are based.

Pondering Points

- In 2019 the UK removed the citizenship of Shamima Begum. As a 15-year-old Shamima had been groomed by online groups to travel to Syria and join ISIS. She soon found herself the bride of terrorist fighters and fled to escape the fighting. As her parents are of Bangladeshi ancestry, the UK government argued that she is not stateless and can, therefore, be stripped of her citizenship. Others have argued that she was a minor when she made the wrong choice, and therefore, the state should be more lenient. What do you think? Should citizenship be taken away from those who support terrorist organisations or commit terrorism? What if they are minors?

- Some have argued that birthplace is a matter of luck which is not fair. What if every child was given a passport by luck? When you are born, your citizenship is chosen by luck, and when you are 18 you have to migrate to that country. Would you find this a good system?
- If you are adopted out of the country your biological parents are from, should you get your biological parent's citizenship? What about children conceived via donors through IVF – should the citizenship of the biological donors be given to the child?

References

Appiah, Kwame Anthony. *Cosmopolitanism: Ethics in a World of Strangers*. New York: W. W. Norton & Company, 2006.

Arendt, Hannah. "The Rights of Man: What Are They?" *Modern Review* 3 (1949): 24–37.

Arendt, Hannah. *The Origins of Totalitarianism*. New York: Harcourt, Brace & Co., 1951.

Balderrama, Francisco E., and Raymond Rodriguez. *Decade of Betrayal: Mexican Repatriation in the 1930s*. Revised ed. Albuquerque: University of New Mexico Press, 2006.

Berlin Wall Museum. "Balloon Escape from the GDR." *The Wall Museum*. www.thewallmuseum.com/en/balloon-escape-from-the-gdr/. (Accessed June 27, 2024).

Byrne, Richard. "The Migrant Labour Shortage Is Already Here – and Agri-Tech Can't Yet Fill the Gap." *LSE Brexit Blog*, January 5, 2018. www.blogs.lse.ac.uk/brexit/2018/01/05/the-migrant-labour-shortage-is-already-here-and-agri-tech-cant-yet-fill-the-gap/.

Carens, Joseph H. *The Ethics of Immigration*. Oxford: Oxford University Press, 2013.

Carrington, Damian. "Lack of Migrant Workers Left Food Rotting in UK Fields Last Year, Data Reveals." *The Guardian*, February 9, 2018. www.theguardian.com/environment/2018/feb/09/lack-of-migrant-workers-left-food-rotting-in-uk-fields-last-year-data-reveals.

Daniels, Roger. *Prisoners Without Trial: Japanese Americans in World War II*. Revised ed. New York: Hill and Wang, 2004.

Dumont, Gérard-François. The Berlin Wall: Life, Death and the Spatial Heritage of Berlin (Le Mur de Berlin: Vie, mort et héritage géopolitique), November 6, 2009. https://ssrn.com/abstract=2361024 or http://dx.doi.org/10.2139/ssrn.2361024.

Economist. "If America Is Overrun by Low-Skilled Migrants." *The Economist*, July 27, 2017. www.economist.com/united-states/2017/07/27/if-america-is-overrun-by-low-skilled-migrants.

Gentleman, Amelia. *The Windrush Betrayal: Exposing the Hostile Environment.* London: Guardian Faber Publishing, 2019.

Hoffman, Abraham. *Unwanted Mexican Americans in the Great Depression: Repatriation Pressures, 1929–1939.* Tucson: University of Arizona Press, 1974.

Kerber, Linda K. "The Stateless as the Citizen's Other: A View from the United States." *American Historical Review* 112 (2007): 1–34.

Ngai, Mae M. *Impossible Subjects: Illegal Aliens and the Making of Modern America.* Princeton: Princeton University Press, 2004.

Rosales, F. Arturo. "Repatriation of Mexicans from the US." In *The Praeger Handbook of Latino Education in the U.S,* edited by Lourdes Diaz Soto, 400–403. Westport, CT: Greenwood Publishing Group, 2007.

van der Vossen, Bas, and Jason Brennan. In *Defense of Openness: Why Global Freedom Is the Humane Solution to Global Poverty.* Oxford, 2018. [Online] https://doi.org/10.1093/oso/9780190462956.001.0001. (Accessed August 17, 2024).

Should We Eat a Guest or 3-D Print Sushi?

Questions About Nature and
Technology

12 Should Nature Have Rights?

Discussing How Humans Relate to Nature

A group of philosophers has come together in our party. They come from a variety of countries – Vandana Shiva from India, Alberto Acosta and Atawallpa Oviedo from Ecuador, Australian Peter Singer, American Christopher Stone, and Bruno Latour from France. Their conversation is lively. Latour taps a fork on his glass to get the attention of the whole room.

Acosta speaks up – 'We have been chatting here among friends, and we agree that our conversation is limited, not just limited but rather mistaken, if we speak only of the interest of humans. Putting humans in the centre of politics is what has led to an economy, a society, that is destructive, non-sustainable, and damaging. We need to re-think the rules we create, the societies we are building, and start by consider the rights of all. Not just the rights of all humans, but the rights of all nature'.

A cheer raises from the philosophers who stand around Acosta.

'I am not sure I understand' states, confused, Francis Bacon, a seventeenth-century English philosopher. 'Nature is men's dominion, to control and use for our advancement'.

'No', responds Vandana Shiva, 'that is the Western perspective that has gotten us in so much trouble. It has led us to use and abuse nature to the point of destruction. But in ancestral cultures, we do not see nature as something we control. We see nature as something we are part of and which we must respect – much as we would take care of our arm to take care of ourselves'.

'In the Andes', adds Atawallpa, 'we have the concept of *Sumak Kawsay* which means 'to live well' and it includes the lives of all things. We cannot live well if our brothers are suffering. We cannot live well when our rivers are polluted, killing the fish. We cannot live well if our planet is dying.'

One of the ways to think about political philosophy is as a bubble of rights. Many of the debates in political philosophy have been around (pun intended) who should be in the bubble. At one point in the West, it was only white property-owning men who were in the centre of the bubble, this expanded to most men, then to most men and women … what about

DOI: 10.4324/9781032620121-16

> bringing animals and plants into this bubble? What about looking at other cultures, who have sought to defend the lives, dignity, and rights of non-human creatures?

You are at the zoo. You are in awe, watching an immense gorilla walk around, its muscles flexing with every step. Gorillas are an endangered species, and you think how sad it is to be watching what might be one of the last of these impressive creatures. Suddenly a little boy decides he wants a better view and scrambles to get on top of the barrier that separates you from the gorilla enclosure. He manages to pull himself up and, before you can say anything, falls into the gorilla enclosure, landing in a small pond with a great splash. You scream.

Everyone rushes to see what happened and starts screaming for help. The little boy, frightened, sits up, soaked, and starts crying. A gorilla rushes over and plucks the boy out of the water as though he were a feather. Everyone screams louder. The gorilla looks around, confused by all the noise. The little boy is now too frightened to cry and sits trembling in the gorilla's hands.

What do you think should happen next?

The zoo could wait and see what the gorilla does with the little boy. The zookeeper could try to lure the gorilla to see its trainer and bring the boy back. Or the zoo could decide to shoot the gorilla – a tranquilizer or a deadly weapon could be used. What do you think would be best?

When a very similar scenario took place in real life, the zoo chose to kill the gorilla and save the little boy. The family of the little boy was, of course, relieved and thankful that their boy had been saved. But some asked – was this the most ethical choice?

There are only a few gorillas left on the planet. There are billions of little boys. While the boy was unique and precious to his family … we could argue that the gorilla was also precious and unique to his family. The gorilla, moreover, is also precious to the planet, as one of the few that could continue the existence of its species. Do the lives of humans and gorillas have the same value, or are humans more valuable … or are gorillas' lives more valuable because there are fewer gorillas? In 1993 philosophers Peter Singer and Paola Cavalieri launched the 'Great Ape Project' which argued that great apes, given their cognitive and emotional capacities, should be granted basic rights including the right to life, liberty, and protection from torture.

The gorilla, moreover, had done nothing bad – it could even be argued that it saved the boy from drowning. On the other hand, the little boy had invaded the gorilla's house uninvited and caused great chaos, stressing the gorilla for no reason. If there was a criminal in this situation, in other words, it was the little boy, not the gorilla.

Yet, letting a little boy be hurt by a gorilla is a horrible idea to consider. Why?

Speciesism and Religion

Psychologist and philosopher Richard D. Ryder would argue this is a case of *speciesism*. Humans think of ourselves as the most precious species, place our own species above others, and consider our pain more important. Humans, therefore, will kill any animal that threatens one of our species, even if the animal is an innocent bystander of human actions.

This speciesism is supported by certain religions and cultures which see humans as the most valuable specie because, for example, they believe humans holds the spirit of God. Some interpretations of Christianity, for instance, argue that the Bible states that God made man to rule over all of nature, and breathed His spirit only into humans, not other species.

This is not a universal view, however. Other cultures and religions hold the spirit of god, or gods, as existing in other parts of nature or in all parts of nature. In the Andes, for example, nature is *Pacha Mama*, or Mother Earth, allowing births and life, and causing earthquakes. In Andean cosmology humans are part of nature, they are not above nature and not made to rule it. Whenever a person takes something from nature, they need to thank nature and give something back.

Sumak Kawsay

Indigenous peoples, whose lifestyle requires a much closer interaction with nature than that of city-dwellers (who might only see nature as glimpses of the sky in between tall buildings) have argued that humans need to change how they relate to nature. Following the leadership of indigenous people, for example, the governments of Ecuador and Bolivia have put the concept of *sumac kawsay* in their national constitutions. *Sumac Kawsay* means *good life* in Kichwa but this good life means good not just for humans but good for all living things. As Alberto Acosta explains, this means rethinking how we live so that nature is not just something we use, and not something we can buy and sell, but something we are part of and protect.

This philosophy lines up with what has become known as *doughnut economics*. Doughnut economics, an idea proposed by Kate Raworth, argues that when we build our world, we need to try to live within two limits – which you can think of as two sides of a doughnut. The inner side is the social foundation, what humans need to survive well and justly (this includes not just basics like water and food, but also education, equality, voice), and the outer part of the doughnut is our environmental limit. When we go beyond the top, we break the doughnut and start to destroy the environment.

However, doughnut economics and *sumac kawsay* are not the same. Doughnut economics notes that we need nature to survive, so we need to respect nature for our benefit. Sumac Kawsay sees nature as deserving respect on its own right, not just because it is an instrument for our survival. Nature is intrinsically, not just instrumentally, valuable. This is an important difference as it moves us away from speciesism toward seeing ourselves as part of nature, not as a special species.

Human as an Ecosystem?

You might be having a snack while you read this book. Suddenly your stomach lets out a loud sound. That tenth carrot was probably not a good idea. 'Something in your gut seems unhappy', your brother says. 'Ha!' you laugh at the expression, 'Imagine if someone actually lived in my gut and I just fed it 10 carrots and 5 doughnuts'.

Well, the truth is, someone does live in your gut. In fact, a lot of 'someones' do. About 100 trillion. These little bacteria are an integral part of you. If you got rid of them, your health would be undermined. These bacteria help you digest your food, they help you synthesise vitamin K, they help promote the formation of new blood vessels, and protect you from infections. And they are not the only beings that live on you – and without whom you would struggle. For example, you also have little mites that live in your face, eating dead skin cells – now that is a pleasant thought!

Your gut biome is particularly interesting.[1] Research appears to show that what bacteria inhabits your gut affects your brain, influencing how you feel, how you act.[2] This brings us back to questions of who you are. If your feelings are affected by your gut bacteria – are these bacteria part of you? Perhaps you are not just a 'single human' but a small ecosystem, an entity that is the result of trillions of bacteria populating a variety of cells, that results in what you think of, and feel, as you.

Most of the research on what is being called the gut-brain axis has been undertaken on other animals. Mice without gut bacteria, for example, have been found to be more anxious. If we think about the implications of this research, we are forced to rethink what living creatures are – and what we are.[3] We are not independent beings – neither human nor other animals – we are creatures that are made up by smaller creatures, trillions of small creatures we are not even aware of, but who affect whether, and how, we live or die. Thinking of ourselves as a separate species is perhaps short sighted, illogical, and unethical? Perhaps we need to respect nature because we *are* nature: we are a combination of many small creatures that create each of us.

The Rights of Nature

Will you give bacteria rights?

What does this even mean? Can you imagine the trillion of microbes in your body holding placards that say 'Antibiotics kill the good guys too! No antibiotics!'

The idea that nature should have rights is quite fascinating. Nature has been given rights in law by some governments. Ecuador became the first country to give nature rights in its 2008 constitution which states 'Nature, or Pacha Mama, where life is reproduced and occurs, has the right to integral respect for its existence and for the maintenance and regeneration of its life cycles, structure, functions and evolutionary processes' (Article 71).

However, we need to go back and think about what this means – and what nature is. We might agree, for example, that air pollution is not good and, therefore, for example, using fireworks could be seen as going against the rights of nature. However, does all of nature get the same rights?

Let's go back to your gut biome, for a moment. When we realise that these bacteria are part of our being and need to remain alive for us to be alive, we might consider that bacteria should also be given rights – after all, we could see these rights as our right – as we cannot live well without the bacteria. But we kill bacteria on a daily basis. We spray antibacterial spray on surfaces. We wash our hands. And we take antibiotics. Should all of these activities be stopped?

Those who follow Jainism believe that all life is precious, and some very devout Jains might walk carefully sweeping the floor in front of them to avoid stepping on any small critter. They believe that killing any living thing will create negative karma.

This belief, however, runs into problems when we consider public health. Should malaria carrying mosquitos, for example, be allowed to live and infect humans, or should we use pesticides to kill them? Or let's talk about growing food. I once planted a small garden with kale and broccoli. Then I saw a small green caterpillar on a kale leaf. I thought the caterpillar was endearing: carefully and assiduously chewing with its tiny mouth. So I left it, thinking we could share the garden, the tiny caterpillar and me. He was so small; he would surely be happy with a couple of leaves, and I would get to see the beautiful butterfly it would turn into. A couple of days later I returned ... to find hundreds of caterpillars eating the last bits of what was once my garden. I was left without a single leaf. To add salt to the wound, the caterpillars never turned into beautiful butterflies. I saw nothing but one pale, unattractive moth a few weeks later. I was not dependant on that kale to survive, but if I was a farmer, losing my whole crop would have been a disaster. It could have meant starvation for me and many others. I would have killed those caterpillars.

When growing food, farmers need to decide how to manage pests that threaten their crop. Organic farming can include encouraging certain insects that can eat other insects, those that threaten crops. While this might not be the same as, say, killing bugs with pesticide, it still implies supporting one life force and letting others die. Is this what giving rights to nature means? Giving rights to one bug to eat another?

How can we give right to nature, when the interests of one part of nature – such as slugs – run against the interests of other parts – such as lettuce? Should we have a vote and see if lettuce or slugs get more votes? While there is clearly no single answer to how nature should be represented, philosophers argue that this is not an unsurmountable problem. Legal philosopher Christopher Stone, for example, asked why if companies, which are fully inanimate things, are represented in court and are given a 'legal' personhood, why can't the same be done for nature? Bruno Latour argues that scientists could help us understand the needs of nature – they could interpret nature's needs and present these to a court of justice. Nature would have a voice, it would no longer be simply used by and for humans, it would be considered fairly whenever changes were considered. Just like with humans in court, the choice of the court might not always make everyone happy, but at least nature would get a hearing.

Testing the Rights of Nature

There are several examples that we can use to think through the rights of nature. We could consider, for example, whether animals should be used for testing or in war. The history of medicine and cosmetics has a dark history as lots of the products we now use were once tested for safety on other animals – such as mice, rats, rabbits, and dogs. Space travel owes great debts to little animals launched into orbit. These animals, of course, did not consent to these experiments and many suffered terribly. Equally in war, animals valiantly galloped to their deaths, or were shot down when carrying messages. However, the question often asked is, would it have been better to not run these experiments, not to use these animals? If we did not, many diseases would still be untreatable, and many humans might have had terribly painful or deadly experiences. Again, we see speciesism and anthropocentrism: putting humans at the centre of our decision making, choosing based on human interests.[4]

Conclusion

The challenge of this chapter is whether we can move away from speciesism, away from anthropocentrism to a perspective that values nature as much as we value ourselves. Arne Naess has coined the term deep ecology as a way to think of humans as just one of the precious life forms in our planet. I wonder if we look beyond our planet, if we ever encounter an extra-terrestrial life form – what rights would we give it? What rights would it give us?

Chapter Summary

Should nature have rights? This chapter has considered whether it is ethically correct for humans to base their choices solely on the interests of humans (an anthropocentric perspective) or whether we should move to an ecocentric per-spective, a deep ecology, as Arne Naess called for, where humans are seen as just one of the many life forms that seek to survive in our planet. This is a move away from speciesism, a term created by Richard D. Ryder to label our tendency to think humans as more important than other species. This discussion enters into religious debates as well – as some religions present humans as the only holders of God's spirit and other religions present some or all of nature as inhabited by god/gods.

Giving nature rights is not as unthinkable as it might initially appear. Ecuador was the first state to officially give nature rights in its constitution, but well before that Peter Singer and Paola Cavalieri launched the Great Apes Project to advocate granting great apes rights. Christopher Stone had previously argued that since corporations are given legal personhood there is no reason for nature to lack this. Bruno Latour argued that scientists could act as spokespeople for nature. Giving nature rights might ultimately be in our interests, as humans are not independent entities but small ecosystems that depend for their survival on trillions of microbes that inhabit us.

Pondering Points

- If a human could be sacrificed to save the lives of 20 other animals (any animal you chose), would this be morally right? What if sacrificing one human could save an entire animal species?
- Let's think about the ethics of genetic modification. Is modifying the make-up of nature inherently against its rights? Genetic modification has been used to create animals and plants that are stronger, more resistant to disease and plagues. Could we argue that genetic modification is in the interests of nature?
- How can we balance the rights of nature and cultural rights? If a culture uses animals/plants as part of sacred ceremonies, should they stop?

References

Acosta, Alberto, and Mateo Martínez Abarca. "Buen Vivir: An Alternative Perspective from the Peoples of the Global South to the Crisis of Capitalist Modernity." In *The Climate Crisis: South African and Global Democratic Eco-Socialist Alternatives*, edited by Vishwas Satgar, 131–147. Johannesburg: Wits University Press, 2018.

Anonye, Blessing. "Gut Bacteria and Its Role in Human Health." www.warwick.ac.uk/newsandevents/knowledgecentre/science/life-sciences/gut_bacteria/. (Accessed April 2, 2024).

Bacon, Francis. *Novum Organum*. Edited and translated by Peter Urbach and John Gibson. Chicago: Open Court, 1994/1620. Book 1, Aph. CXXIX.

Constitución de la República del Ecuador. Registro Oficial 449, 20 October 2008.

Draper, Chris. "Gorilla in the Midst of a Zoo Fog." *Journal of Animal Welfare Law* (Summer 2016). www.bornfree.org.uk/storage/media/content/files/Publications/ Opinion__Gorilla_in_the_midst_of_a_zoo_fog.pdf.

Johnson, Katerina V.-A. "Gut Microbiome Composition and Diversity Are Related to Human Personality Traits." *Human Microbiome Journal* 15 (2020): 100069. https:// doi.org/10.1016/j.humic.2019.100069.

Latour, Bruno. *Politics of Nature: How to Bring the Sciences into Democracy.* Translated by Catherine Porter. Cambridge, MA: Harvard University Press, 2004.

Naess, Arne. "The Shallow and the Deep, Long-Range Ecology Movement. A Summary." *Inquiry* 16, no. 1–4 (1973): 95–100.

NPR. "Gorilla Killed to Save Boy at Cincinnati Zoo." *NPR: The Two-Way,* May 29, 2016. www.npr.org/sections/thetwo-way/2016/05/29/479919582/gorilla-killed-to-save-boy-at-cincinnati-zoo.

Oviedo Freire, Atawallpa. *Qué es el sumakawsay: Más allá del socialismo y capitalismo.* Quito: Sumak Editores, 2011.

Raworth, Kate. *Doughnut Economics: Seven Ways to Think Like a 21st-Century Economist.* White River Junction, VT: Chelsea Green Publishing, 2017.

Ryder, Richard D. "Speciesism Again: The Original Leaflet." *Critical Society* 2 (2010): 1–2.

Shiva, Vandana. *Staying Alive: Women, Ecology and Development.* London: Zed Books, 1988.

Singer, Peter. *The Expanding Circle: Ethics, Evolution, and Moral Progress.* Princeton: Princeton University Press, 2011.

Singer, Peter, and Paola Cavalieri, eds. *The Great Ape Project: Equality Beyond Humanity.* New York: St. Martin's Press, 1996.

Stone, Christopher D. "Should Trees Have Standing?—Toward Legal Rights for Natural Objects." *Southern California Law Review* 45 (1972): 450–501.

Villalba, Unai. "Buen Vivir vs Development: A Paradigm Shift in the Andes?" *Third World Quarterly* 34, no. 8 (2013): 1427–1442.

Weismantel, Mary. "Ayllu: Real and Imagined Communities in the Andes." In *The Seductions of Community,* edited by G. Creed, 77–88. Santa Fe: School of American Research Press, 2006.

13 Is Having Pets Immoral?

Discussing Our Favourite Animals

We are in the middle of discussing what basic rules are necessary for humans to live in peace when my Cocker spaniel dog runs into the room, dripping wet from rolling around muddy puddles. Without thinking twice, he stands in the middle of the room and shakes, covering all the philosophers around him with a layer of rain, mud, and some slobber. (Except for Socrates, who very quickly jumps behind Marx and avoids most of the mud).

'What is this beast doing in here?' roars Descartes. 'Put him out', he approaches grumpily, planning to kick my dog back out into the rain. Before I can say anything, Jeremy Bentham stands up and says 'Why, it is miserable outside, you do not intend to send the little creature back out into the cold? Would you like to be stranded out there?'

'Well certainly not! But he is a beast, after all, and I am not! What does it know about being wet or dry?'

'But he can also feel, he can also suffer, surely he deserves to be inside warm and safe[1]?'

I smile my quick thanks to Bentham and quickly cover my wet dog with a towel and send him to another room to finish drying off.

While Bentham argued that animals can feel, historically western philosophers have not considered humans and non-human animals as similar in any way. The idea of keeping pets inside the house safe and warm, might have seen unnecessary to many, and downright disgusting to some.

Let's make believe you have a pet. You can choose what this pet is. It could be a goofy dog. Or a fluffy guinea pig. Or a pig, not particularly cuddly, but pink and round. Or a muscular, slithering, sinuous, snake.

You are occupied taking care of your pet – petting it, feeding it, cleaning its crate, when you realise it is looking at you. No, I mean, really *looking* at you. It

DOI: 10.4324/9781032620121-17

is a bit disconcerting. It is staring at you. You smile, feeling a bit silly at feeling judged by your pet. To your great surprise your pet starts speaking to you! (This is particularly incredible if your pet is a fish – we will just have to assume it creates speech bubbles that emerge from the water.)

'Why?', it asks.

'Why? What? What why? I mean, what are you asking? Wait, you can talk?!'

'Yes, of course I can talk. I can think. I can feel. I can do many things. But I cannot choose. I did not choose to be here. You chose me. I live here in your house, your rules, your schedule, my whole life. Why? Why did you choose me? Why am I here?'

You stand there with your mouth open. Looking a bit like a fish. Not only is it incredible that your pet is speaking out loud … it is also asking some heavy questions.

Do pets want to be pets? Are pets happy? Perhaps, if they had a choice, they would rather be outside, in the wild, rather than living in cities, in houses, by human rules.

If you think about it more broadly – do humans have the right to simply walk into any part of nature, take a living being and call it theirs? Here, for example, is a cat with her kittens. I am just going to take one of her babies to my home because it is so soft and beautiful … what right do we have to do this?

Humans and Non-Human Animals

For as long as there have been humans, we have benefited from other animals by using their bodies for food, clothing, protection, and weapons. This use of animals for our survival can be questioned in terms of justice. Is it right to kill and use other creatures to survive? Vegans argue that we no longer need to kill and use animals for our survival. We can clothe ourselves with plant products and can survive by eating a plant-based diet. Why, then, should we unnecessarily kill other beings or even use them for our benefit?

The more we understand about other animals the more the idea of killing them or using them becomes problematic. For René Descartes, a French philosopher who lived in the seventeenth century, animals were furry machines, bête-machine or 'beast machines'.[2] Since he thought animals were just mechanical devices that lacked reason or a soul, Descartes had no problem taking them apart to investigate the structures of their bodies. He did not consider their pain or suffering – and assumed any sound they made was just a mechanical noise. A century later Jeremy Bentham opposed practices that hurt animals, not because he thought they could think like humans, but because they could feel pain. Thus, he said 'The question is not, can they reason? nor, can they talk? but, can they suffer?'[3]

However, we now understand that animals do indeed feel pain, but more than that they can reason, have a sense of self, and demonstrate empathy and creativity. We know that great apes are very close to humans in the complexity of their social structures and enjoy games and learning new things. Social media provides anecdotal evidence, with thousands of videos of dogs using speech buttons to communicate complex ideas and feelings. And we have a growing body of research on the creative abilities, intelligence, and emotional capacity of various animals including birds, dolphins and whales, elephants, and bunnies.[4] This has led academics to launching and signing the New York Declaration on Animal Consciousness which declares:

First, there is strong scientific support for attributions of conscious experience to other mammals and to birds.

Second, the empirical evidence indicates at least a realistic possibility of conscious experience in all vertebrates (including reptiles, amphibians, and fishes) and many invertebrates (including, at minimum, cephalopod mollusks, decapod crustaceans, and insects).

Third, when there is a realistic possibility of conscious experience in an animal, it is irresponsible to ignore that possibility in decisions affecting that animal. We should consider welfare risks and use the evidence to inform our responses to these risks.[5]

How can we justify choosing what life these smart, creative, emotional animals should have? Can we justify killing some of them simply to satiate our taste? And can we justify keeping some of them prisoners simply because they are good company?

My Dog Is Not Just an Animal, He Is My Pet

Humans' relationship to pets is different than our relationship to other animals. We keep pets for their company, for their beauty, for their intelligence. Pets are not food or clothing material, they are company, support, and help.

Is it just to make an animal your pet? After all, if someone took you into their house and kept you there because they enjoyed your company you would consider this kidnapping and not a pleasant experience. But this is what we do with pets. We enjoy our pets, but do they enjoy us?

Now, you might be certain your pet loves you. I certainly think our dog loves us. When we come home, he folds himself into doughnuts and offers us treasured shoes in exchange for cuddles. His tail wags so fast that his back legs almost lift off the floor.

But our dog also did not have an option. We picked him when he was a tiny 8-week-old puppy and brought him to our house. We have given him the best life we can think of – full of good food, full of love, and with frolics through the woods which clearly delight him almost as much as peeing on every shrub he can find ... but he never had another option. He has no option but to love us as he depends completely on us. But is that love or desperation?

The Creation of Pets

Of course, we might argue that pets could not survive in the wild at this point – so they do not have any option but to be pets. If we opened our doors and let our cats and dogs out, released our guinea pigs and gerbils on the streets, and opened the railings and cages holding birds and reptiles in our houses … we would first have great chaos … and then we would soon find most of these poor animals starved to death or eaten by each other. They are safer with us. They are happier with us, we might therefore say, and pat ourselves on the back.

But this takes us back further, because many of the animals we now see as our pets, would not look, or act, the way they do if humans had not intervened in their breeding and rearing. Wolves would not have naturally evolved into chihuahuas! You can just imagine an ancestral wolf looking at a chihuahua saying, 'Really? I, a fearsome, majestic creature, will turn into a canine-version of a rodent? This is my future if I take handouts from humans?! I give up power and strength … to have googly eyes and be carried in a purse?'

Humans have bred pets for their benefit. Dogs are a particularly clear example of this. If you look at all the amazing breeds of dogs that exist, you will see that each dog has been bred for a different purpose. Some dogs are bred for speed, some for the strength of their bite, some for extra skin, some to hunt badgers. We have bred dogs whose hair we can perm and dye to match our outfits. And we have bred dogs able to fight each other to the death for our amusement. While each type of dog might be cute, or handsome, or amazing, this breeding has also hurt dogs.

We have helped creatures evolve in ways that make them increasingly vulnerable. Pugs, for example, have adorable little faces – which look like the result of running into a wall at full speed – but they struggle to breathe. Dachshunds' long backs which make them look like sausages with an attitude, often result in injured spines that require expensive surgeries or wheelchairs.

As we realise that our desire for long/short/tall/funny dogs might hurt dogs, is it ethical to continue to breed animals for our human desires? Would it not be more ethical to allow animals to breed freely, allowing genetic diversity?

You might know that some breeds of dogs have been banned in different countries, particularly those perceived as too dangerous for humans. However, why do we decide what dogs can be bred or not based on what is good for us, for humans, rather than what is good for the dogs? Yet, if we want to breed what is best for the animal – how can we decide that? Would we aim for a longer life, more genetic diversity, a dog that is closer to its wolf ancestors? Should we even have the right to decide what is 'best' for another species?

A Lonely Life and a Sad End

During the Covid-19 pandemic the demand for pets increased. People felt alone and bored at home and sought company in pets. Demand for dogs increased.

When selling dogs became more profitable, more dogs were bred, with thousands of young puppies being born. Many of these found loving homes, but many of them did not. Is it right to bring animals into existence just to sell them to humans?

As people went back to their normal schedule after pandemic lockdowns, many pets found themselves suddenly home alone. It is ironic that we get pets for our company, but force pets into lonely lives. Many pets spend most of their life alone inside a house, waiting for humans to come and give them food and a bit of attention. Is this a fair way to treat these creatures?

Those unable to care for their pets might choose to give them up, hoping someone else can adopt them. This is itself a traumatic experience for pets – imagine suddenly losing everything you knew and being taken by people you have never seen before. Moreover, the reality is that there are more pets looking for homes than people looking for pets and many little animals end up suffering and lonely in their last days. Many animals are put down, unable to find a new home to care for them.

There are clearly several ethical issues here. Who is responsible for these animals that we breed, use, abandon, and sometimes kill? Should animals be sold as goods? There is a market for these pets – people who breed and sell pets. However, when the market miscalculates how many pets are wanted, or for how long, we are not talking about unwanted bicycles or cars that are left on the lot. We are talking about intelligent, caring beings that are left unwanted, without any choice in the matter. Perhaps the sale of animals should be illegal. Or perhaps we need to stop thinking of animals as property and see them as vulnerable creatures who deserve consideration and care. In their book *Zoopolis* (2011) philosophers Sue Donaldson and Will Kymlicka argue that we should think of domestic animals as co-citizens – they are an intrinsic part of our life, and us of theirs, thus, our government, our rules, should consider them as part of our social contract.[6]

The Cost of Pets

Pets also affect the existence of other animals. Every animal affects the food chain around it. Domestic cats decimate native birds. Cats are hunters, that is their nature. And cats like to roam their neighbourhood. By having cats as pets, we are setting loose millions of little hunters in our neighbourhood. We are grateful if they hunt down pests, but what about when they hunt down robins, cardinals, lovely little birds that might be endangered and which we love to be surrounded by? Less birds means more insects ... and the imbalance increases.

The cost of pets shows up in other ways. What do we feed our pets? Feeding pets requires food, of course, and growing food takes energy. The food that we grow for animals is food that we do not grow for other humans. The food that we grow for animals takes up space, and energy, and causes pollution. You might look at a map of South America, for example, and see how many trees have been cut down to make way for grain farming, to feed cattle and pets. Feeding pets has an environmental impact.[7]

Some pets, however, are not fed processed food but other animals. Some snakes, for example, are fed rodents. Imagine a room full of soft little squeaking mice … the destiny of these furry little beings is to be packaged and sold to feed someone's pet python. While it is the law of nature that some must die for others to live, is it different if we bring thousands of lives into existence just to be fed to others? The mice bred to feed snakes have no opportunity to experience a different life. If there were no pet snakes, they might not have been bred at all.

Ending Pet Ownership

As you can see the topic of pets brings up some serious ethical considerations. Should we own animals? Are we responsible for providing animals with a good life? What is a good life for a pet? We have also considered the ecological cost of pets, and the fact that pet ownership leads to the deaths of other animals. Ultimately, the underlying question is should we own pets at all?

Some philosophers, such as Gary Francione, have argued that the only correct option is to end pet ownership. Clearly, this cannot be done suddenly. Animals who are already our pets cannot simply be returned to the wild. Pet ownership can only be stopped over time and with the support of governments.

Would this apply to support animals? Some pets have incredible abilities. There are pets who can sniff, for example, when a person's insulin is too high or too low and tell them so they can correct the imbalance before they go into diabetic shock. Some pets can help people who are blind navigate cities safely. Some pets can give comfort and support to individuals suffering with mental health issues or those grieving. Would it be just to also get rid of these pets given the important role they play for their humans?

Again, the answer is not simple. Yet, we are again considering the needs of humans first. What impact, for example, does it have for a pet to support a person in distress? Can giving such support lead to stress or discomfort for the pet? Should this be considered?

Clearly, one of the challenges here is that we still have far to go toward understanding what animals want and what they feel. We can assume what they want, but we do this from our human perspective. Is it possible for us to understand the world from a non-human perspective?[8]

Cloning Our Pets

Scientific advances can also affect how we relate to our pets. For example, if you are willing to pay enough you might never need to say goodbye to your pet. Well almost.

We are talking here about cloning your pet. As your pet ages and you are facing the reality of their mortality, would you consider cloning your pet to have a new pet that is as much of your current pet as possible?

Some people have opted to do this, and cloning pets is an emerging business. But again, we are faced with choices that put the desires of humans before the desires or well-being of any other animal (we can be fairly certain that no animal 'wants' to be cloned). Cloning does not benefit the pets in any way. In fact, the process of cloning requires a variety of painful, or at least uncomfortable, medical procedures on animals who are used to create and grow the new pet. How can we justify the use of these animals as carriers of our cloned pet? These animals face risks and discomfort for our benefit, not theirs.

I also find the idea of cloning a pet curious in other ways. To start with, it assumes that two entities with almost identical genes would be the same – this would only be the case if all that our pets are were their genes.[9] But what about their experiences with us? Does that not shape who they are and how they relate to us?

Moreover, if we are just trying to re-create the pet we already had, how are we going to relate to this new, cloned pet? The cloned pet will be a new animal, a new creature, but will we try to treat it like the pet who died? Clearly that would not respect this new pet's uniqueness. It would be valuing the pet only for being like another being, not for its unique self. This cannot be just. Imagine if your parents only liked you for how much you are like them. They applaud every time you do something they would do but get annoyed or confused when you do something that makes you, well, you. This would not be love toward you, it would be destructive and unfair.

Surely the ultimate argument for having pets is that we can love and care for them as unique beings. That we treasure their lives and love them. But if we clone a pet, our relationship with the clone would start with a failed position as we are not loving them, but loving the memory of the being they were cloned from.

Conclusion

Humans' relationship with animals is evolving.[10] At one point some philosophers thought of animals as nothing more than furry machines. Many still think of pets as disposable goods one can buy and abandon as needed. Yet, the more we know about other animals, the more such views and behaviour stand as unethical. While we might never know what it is like to be a bat, or a cat, or a dog, we can empathise with creatures that can think, feel, and create like us. This empathy prompts us to consider what is a just way to treat animals, to ask whether having pets is just and what is the most just way to treat our pets. I will stop this chapter now and go play with my dog to try and bring more joy into his life.

Chapter Summary

This chapter has considered whether having pets is ethical. We have explored how Western understanding of animals' abilities and rights has changed, from Descartes's view of animals as machines, to Bentham's view of animals as feeling creatures, to Donaldson and Kymlicka's view that animals should be considered co-citizens and thus considered when we make rules to govern our society. We have also noted that some philosophers, such as Francione, argue for the end of pet ownership, as treating animals as property is inherently unfair to their autonomy. We considered the market for pets and whether breeding, buying, and cloning animals for the benefit of humans could ever be just, with a special note on animals that help humans survive, such as medical aid dogs. We also considered other hidden impacts of pets, such as the ecological impact of domestic cats and the environmental impact of producing food for pets. We considered the fact that pet ownership encourages the breeding of other animals to feed our pets, and wondered what rights humans have not just to own, but to demand the life and death of other animals.

Pondering Points

- Should pet owners be required to pass an application before getting a pet? Does this include pets such as snails?
- Should pet ownership be phased out?
- In a previous chapter we mentioned zoos. Should zoos remain – as places to safeguard precious animals raising awareness about them – or are these places of torture for animals which should be free?

References

Andrews, K., J. Birch, J. Sebo, and T. Sims. "Background to the New York Declaration on Animal Consciousness." nydeclaration.com, 2024.

Bentham, Jeremy. *An Introduction to the Principles of Morals and Legislation*. United Kingdom: Hafner Publishing Company, 1948/1789.

Birch, Jonathan, Charlotte Burn, Alexandra Schnell, Heather Browning, and Andrew Crump. "Review of the Evidence of Sentience in Cephalopod Molluscs and Decapod Crustaceans." *London School of Economics and Political Science* (November 2021). www.lse.ac.uk/business/consulting/assets/documents/Sentience-in-Cephalopod-Molluscs-and-Decapod-Crustaceans-Final-Report-November-2021.pdf.

Croney, Candace C. "Turning up the Volume on Man's Best Friend: Ethical Issues Associated with Commercial Dog Breeding." *Journal of Applied Animal Ethics Research* 1, no. 2 (2019): 230–252.

Descartes, René. *Discourse on Method and Meditations on First Philosophy*. Translated by Donald A. Cress. 4th ed. Indianapolis: Hackett Publishing Company, 1998/1637.

Donaldson, Sue, and Will Kymlicka. *Zoopolis: A Political Theory of Animal Rights*. United Kingdom: OUP Oxford, 2011.

Francione, Gary, and Anna Charlton. "The Case Against Pets." *Aeon*, July 19, 2017. www.aeon.co/essays/why-keeping-a-pet-is-fundamentally-unethical.

Gigliotti, Carol. *The Creative Lives of Animals*. United States: NYU Press, 2022.

Heðinsdóttir, K., S. Kondrup, H. Röcklinsberg, and F. Palmer. "Can Friends be Copied? Ethical Aspects of Cloning Dogs as Companion Animals." *Journal of Agricultural and Environmental Ethics* 31 (2018): 17–29.

Ho, Jeffery, Sabir Hussain, and Olivier Sparagano. "Did the COVID-19 Pandemic Spark a Public Interest in Pet Adoption?" *Frontiers in Veterinary Science* 8 (2021). https://doi.org/10.3389/fvets.2021.647308.

Menor-Campos, D. J. "Ethical Concerns about Fashionable Dog Breeding." *Animals* 14, no. 5 (2024): 756.

Nagel, Thomas. "What Is It Like to Be a Bat?" *The Philosophical Review* 83, no. 4 (October 1974): 435–450.

Pierce, Jessica. *Run, Spot, Run: The Ethics of Keeping Pets*. Chicago: University of Chicago Press, 2016.

14 Would You Like to Become a Cyborg?

Discussing Transhumanism and Posthumanism

What if instead of looking at how to improve our society, we look at how to improve us, as a species. How do we make humans better? Stronger, fitter, smarter! 'What if we use new technology to change human nature?', I ask the philosophers.

'Yes', transhuman philosopher David Pearce speaks up, 'we have an obligation, we *must*, stop all possible suffering. If we can use machines, technology, science, to make our lives better, why wouldn't we? This is what I call the *hedonistic imperative*'.

The idea of avoiding all suffering is, of course, attractive. Some philosophers, like Donna Haraway and Julian Savulescu discuss the possibilities and drawbacks of technology to help humans overcome inequalities, such as those between sexes.

Maurice Merlaeu-Ponty seems interested. '*Allors*', he asks, if we change our body, we would change our perception of the world. It would deeply affect our sense of self and change our understanding of reality.' Phenomenologist philosophers, like Merlaeu-Ponty, argue that we understand change our world through our embodied experiences – that is through our bodies' experiences. Imagine, for example, how different your understanding of the world would be if you were, say, a fish. You would find air dry and suffocating, while water would be soothing and welcoming. Or if you were unable to see colours, or to taste anything sweet.

Technology might be a way for humans to improve ourselves – perhaps we could change our bodies to eat less or to produce less waste – but we have to ask if, and how, these changes might affect how we understand the world as humans.

Imagine if at the supermarket you could buy not just food, but also upgrades for different body parts. You could get an upgrade for your eyeballs – get telescopic or microscopic vision! Or you could get an update for your joints so you could

DOI: 10.4324/9781032620121-18

jump 6 feet straight up into the air and not crack like popcorn. Or maybe a skin upgrade so you could grab boiling hot things without getting burnt!

What would you get?

Let's imagine you decided to spend your money on a new tongue that allows you to taste more flavours! Now you can tell the difference between 80% and 75% dark chocolate without any doubts! And this upgraded tongue is extra-long so you can lick your eyeballs like a reptile.

As you exit, you are surprised to find a group of protestors blocking your path. They are screaming 'Stop the madness, keep humans, human! No alterations to humanity!'. A protestor has a poster of a humanoid robot that reads: 'When does a human stop being a human?'. Someone comes up to you and yells, 'Are you even human anymore?'

What Makes You Human?

The protestors' banners make you think: what is it that makes us human? Is it our body that makes us human? If we change our body, do we become less human?

Humans, however, have been changing their body throughout history. For example, there are many humans who use prosthesis. Technology has advanced so that people who have lost limbs in accidents or due to disease, or who were born with a limb difference, can wear human-made arms, legs, fingers, et cetera, to help them obtain the same mobility as an average person. You can also get a hip replacement if your own hip gives out or breaks, or a pacemaker to help your heart maintain a steady rhythm. Do we think any of these people are not human or wrong for what they have done? Probably not. Yet, somehow, if you told me you wanted to remove your ear and replace it with a bat-like ear to use echolocation … I would consider this different. Why?

Perhaps the difference here is whether a person is changing their body to make it as useful as any other, average, person, or whether we are changing our body to gain abilities far beyond those of even exceptional humans.

Yet surely the use of science to make humans more able is something we should all be happy with. Imagine the possibilities. We might overcome environmental limitations. If we could get gill-like organs, some humans might choose to live under water. Or we might be able to survive in planets that are currently uninhabitable for humanity. Or a single person might be strong enough to build their own house, or so fast that they no longer need to use vehicles to travel long distances.[1]

The idea of expanding or changing what is a human opens incredible possibilities for humanity's future. But, as with all changes, we also face a variety of drawbacks to consider.

Improving Humans – A Dark History

Human history is filled with competition – the search for the fastest runner, the best artist, the greatest thinker. There is, arguably, a good side to this. Competition can inspire us to try harder. On the other hand, competition can be destructive.

War and colonisation are in part a competition, with the winners arguing they are superior to those who lost. Racist arguments stating that light-skinned people were more evolved than other people and therefore *should* conquer and guide these people were presented to support colonisation.[2]

There is no scientific truth behind the idea that people with any skin colour – white,[3] purple, or green – are better than others. There is no scientific truth to the idea of different human 'races'. Science shows that we cannot separate humans into races. Moreover, the idea of 'races' has had terrible consequences when used by governments to 'improve' their population.

The idea that some people are inferior, less evolved, less rational has been used by governments to justify killing, and sterilising others.[4] The idea of 'improving' humans by only supporting the reproduction of those with 'superior' genes is called *eugenics*, a term created by Charles Darwin's half-cousin Francis Galton.[5] Eugenics was employed by the Nazi regime to argue that Jewish people, as well as those considered disabled, those struggling with mental health, and non-heterosexuals, should be killed to cleanse the German population's genes. The idea that non-whites were inferior to whites has been used to justify slavery and conquest. Representing others as non-human is something still present in twenty-first-century conflicts – the enemy is always presented as less than human, less able to feel, less rational. This argument of racial superiority has also been used by countries to justify keeping some migrants out as racially inferior and to justify encouraging the immigration those of 'superior' races.[6]

The idea of improving humanity, therefore, has a dark and bloody history. Yet, one might still argue that it is, in fact, the job of governments to improve their population. Certainly not by killing groups they don't like, but what about by providing food so that children can grow strong and healthy. A government that tries to provide all its population with the best possible food, the best possible medicines, an environment that is healthy, would not be doing something wrong. The difference between population improvement and eugenics lies in inequality and death: eugenics supports only part of the population and is willing to kill those it sees as damaging to the gene stock.

But what if a government gave all of its population surgeries to make them stronger?

Inequality and Change

In 2018 Dr He Jiankui modified the genes of three babies to make them immune to HIV.[7] This action was done without the Chinese government's permission and led to fines and jail time. The genetically modified babies, however, are now alive and prompt questions about whether such procedures should be considered in the future. If you have money and can afford to modify your children to make them healthier, stronger, more intelligent, why shouldn't you?

One of the concerns with using science to 'improve' humans, is who will have access to these improvements. Science is expensive. Very few people will have the resources to edit the genomes of their children. What will happen if only the wealthy can afford technology that makes them stronger, faster, smarter, healthier … Could we have societies divided between a wealthy super-human class, and an underclass?

This division could also take place between countries. If one country is able to modify its citizens to become immune to a particular disease, could this not create a group of super-soldiers when it comes to warfare? Imagine soldiers who are immune to biological weapons, immune even to high temperatures, stronger and faster than any other human. How could any country defend itself against such soldiers? Could genetic modifications become a new aspect of war?

These are, of course, rather far-fetched ideas. But it is the job of philosophers to think about possibilities no matter how distant these might be to try and prepare our society with ethical guidance.

We could look at the other side of the coin. What if we upgraded humans not to be stronger or immune to danger, but more ethical? What if we could insert a machine that gave you a gentle shock when you had a bad thought, or *made* you want to get up and exercise every morning? Psychotherapeutic drugs in a way already do this – they can make us feel less anxious, less depressed, reduce hallucinations. This means we are altering how some humans experience their reality. Is it ethical to intervene in how other humans experience reality, or would it be unethical to let them experience pain or discomfort if we have the drugs and technology to alter these?

Playing God

Unaffected by the protestors at the supermarket you decide to get one more 'human upgrade' at another store. One of the most expensive upgrades allows you to connect your brain to the internet so you can search for information online by just thinking about it. The possibilities are incredible. Imagine how simple any tests would be!

You are about to sign the contract for your upgrade when you notice some tiny print. You ask for a microscope to read it (it is that small!) and read 'As with much cutting-edge science, we cannot predict the long-term effect of this procedure on your brain, your body, or your personality. You undertake this procedure at your own risk. If this procedure makes you dangerous to society, society has the right to end you'.

Well, aren't you glad you read the small print! Would you continue with the procedure?

New technology always carries risk. Changing humans carries great risks. A genetic change might lead to other genetic mutations. Altering our bodies might harm us psychologically in ways we have not yet fully understood – since we have not done this before. Evolution takes time. Technology can allow us, in a way, to bypass this process – rather than wait until we evolve new senses, we can have cameras and search engines inserted into our bodies now! But do we know how this will affect how we feel, how we think, how we teach our children, not just now but in the future?

There are on-going attempts to link our brains to computers. One of the stated goals of these is to allow people with spinal cord injuries to improve their quality of life by controlling machines through their thoughts.[8]

How would you feel about a machine that is part of your body, particularly your brain? While you might initially love having your brain linked to the internet, might it change how you feel about yourself in a few months or a few years? What would happen if the machine crashed?

Bio-Hacking or Taking Science to the People

You leave this second store with your brain unchanged. But apparently while you were inside another group of protestors has found this shop – you seem to attract protestors wherever you go! However, when you look at their signs you realise this is a completely different group. Their signs read:

'Science for all, not just the rich!'

'Let me decide what I want to be!'

One of the protestors hands you a leaflet – 'Join us for a bio-hacking party: making science democratic'.

You might as well visit since you are not getting brain surgery today.

You follow the directions and find yourself in a huge garage converted into a lab. However, this lab is different: it has material and instructions for you to learn how to try things like genetic modifications at home. This is DIY cyborg-making.

Bio-hacking is the idea that we can change our biology to make ourselves better off. Some of those who are interested in bio-hacking argue that the ability to make ourselves stronger, or simply different, should be something that every person can choose to do, it should not be up to governments. Why, after all, should governments be the ones to decide what procedures are safe, what is ethical and what is not? Why should the government have so much control over our bodies?

Philosopher Michel Foucault argued that it is by controlling our bodies that the government extends its power over us. He calls this *biopower*. As society evolves, the government has expanded its control over populations' bodies as a way to expand its power. You can think about this in terms of how the government registers births, makes dietary recommendations, taxes cigarettes, and also approves or disapproves drugs. Bio-hacking can be seen as a way to take biopower back to the people: each person should have complete power to change their body as they wish: from taking vitamins to genetic modification.

At this bio-hacking party some people are listening to a lecture on how to do genetic testing at home. Others are having LEDs and microchips implanted in different parts of their bodies. Some of these are just for fun – because who does not want shiny patterns on their tummy – but some seem rather useful. A few people have their hands wired to open their houses or to be linked to their bank cards – they never have to worry about forgetting their wallets again. Then again, you are troubled by people choosing to remove their eyelids so they can never sleep again – this seems like a terrible idea. Should someone stop them?

You wonder if people should be able to alter their body as they wish, take whatever medicines they want … or whether the government or someone should supervise these actions. Should you have the freedom to try to become a superhuman if you wish? But what if the attempt goes terribly wrong and instead of becoming stronger and faster … you grow a tail and scales and melt your bones? Should society then be responsible to care for this slug-like version of you? Or if you grow unable to manage your temper – like a full-time Hulk – does society need to let you continue to live, even if you are a threat to all those around you?

Rights of Cyborgs

One of the people you meet at the bio-hacking convention convinces you to get an implant that allows you to see in the dark as well as most cats. However, a few years down the road the government decides this machine is dangerous and you get a letter telling you it must be removed. Removal, however, is not only dangerous but you cannot imagine being without this implant anymore, it has become a part of how you understand the world. Before you can decide what to do, the company that came up with the vision technology decide to shut down the software for you and several other cyborgs with other brain implants. You wake up one day in terrible shock as you suddenly cannot see as you are used to. For other cyborgs it is worse. They experience terrible pain as their brain misfires due to sudden changes. Should cyborgs, like you, have rights that protect them from having their new parts taken away without their consent?

Neil Harbisson is the first officially recognised cyborg. Neil was born with achromat vision, which means he could only see in shades of grey. In 2004 Neil had an antenna implanted into his skull which transmits audible vibrations in response to electromagnetic radiation. In this way Neil can 'see' colour through vibrations. This antenna was implanted into his skull by anonymous doctors even after the surgery was rejected several times by various government ethics panels. Neil later had to argue with the UK government to have the antennae included in his passport picture as it is now a permanent part of who he is.

Harbisson and Moon Ribas, who has implants that allow her to sense earthquakes through her feet, co-founded the Cyborg Foundation. The foundation argues that cyborgs need to have their rights recognised. These rights include the right to not have their implants taken off, the right to change what they add or take away from their body, the right to be treated as equal to others, the right to have control over their bodies and to have objects implanted into their body considered part of their natural body. This means a company turning off software used by cyborgs, for example, would be committing a crime against their person.

What cyborgs ask us to think about is whether the division between human and machine can be overcome. Can we stop thinking of a human with a machine as two separate things, and start to think of the human and the machine as one? This means re-thinking what is human.

Can we think of human as something that goes beyond the human body, that includes mechanical, robotic, parts? In a way, we already do this. We started this chapter by discussing prosthetics. We think of prosthetics as part of a person. Taking away a person's prosthetics would strike most of us as a heinous thing to do. Maybe this is just a matter of degree. As humans use machines more and adapt to new technology, will we come to see ourselves as linked to these machines, as the machines being part of us?[9]

Can We Go Beyond Humans

The bigger question that emerges from this discussion is whether there can be a human 2.0. So far humanity has evolved slowly. But why, philosophers like Max More ask, should we limit ourselves to what nature can do? If we have the knowledge to move humans beyond our biological limitations, why should we stop? Perhaps we can even overcome death with technology?

If humans can gain senses from technology – the ability to see new colours, to sense magnetism, to feel electric fields – why should we deny ourselves these possibilities? These new senses might also help us to experience how other animals see our world, and to give us greater empathy for their experience.

If science can help us avoid suffering – again, why deny this? If science can help us live longer, again, why not see how much we can experience in 150 years of life? Nanorobots can be part of our body and immediately detect the intrusion of bacteria or virus, collect data on our hormones and vitamin levels, help to clean arteries. If our brains are connected to the internet there is no reason to think of our minds as stopping within us. Rather than thinking of ourselves as individuals we could think of ourselves as a super-intelligence – an intelligence we all contribute to and benefit from.[10] My ideas would be immediately available to you and yours to me. We could break the barriers that limit us and gain as a species. We could even, maybe, transcend death mentally: if our minds can be shared, uploaded, taken out of our bodies when these can no longer be kept alive, perhaps we can live in a computer as the ultimate cyborg?

Conclusion – Those Left As 'Normal'

However, if project human 2.0 continues, what will happen to humans 1.0? If you or I choose to not change ourselves, or if we simply cannot afford to participate in the adoption of new technology, what might happen to us? How can we ensure humans are not discriminated against, or simply ignored, in a human 2.0 situation?

There is also a question of ownership. As mentioned before, machines, science, is expensive. Will technology adopted by humans be owned by someone? How will we ensure that whoever owns these machines respects those who use them? Or could the worst-case scenario be one where cyborgs are owned by the machine makers? If the owner is unethical, could we manipulate the cyborgs to act in the owner's interest?

As noted by Donna Haraway, technology might help us overcome inequalities between humans. However, the outcome is not necessarily positive. Technology can also be used to sustain or increase inequalities. It might lead to a downgrading of things that are not 'updated' or 'technical'. Technology is always a double-edged sword.

Chapter Summary

In this chapter we have considered how humanity and technology can interact. We have looked at the idea of transhumanism – that is that humans can be enhanced and changed by technology leading to new ways to be human as discussed by Max More. Cyborgs are an example of transhumanism. We discussed the ethics of altering humans, considering the economic and political inequalities that might limit who can be altered, and inequalities that might be caused by these alterations. We met philosopher Pearce who argues we have an obligation to abolish unnecessary pain – and human modifications might be a powerful way to achieve this. We also discussed whether it should be individuals or the government who decide if or how to change human bodies. The idea of biohacking as a democratisation of health was discussed. Merleau-Ponty, a phenomenologist philosopher, reminds us that our understanding of the world happens through our body. We must, therefore, consider how our understanding of the world would change if we changed our bodies. Donna Haraway reminds us that while technology has great promises, it can also be used as a tool of oppression.

Pondering Points

- In another chapter we discussed Marx's idea that history is the history of struggles between economic classes. Is technology moving us to a world where classes are based on technological access?
- If you were ill and there was some medicine that could save your life, but it could also kill you, would you risk taking this medicine? Imagine the government had not approved the medicine as it was not considered safe enough yet. Would you take the medicine anyway?
- In the case of the babies who were genetically modified an interesting angle is that this modification was done by the parents without the children's consent. Do you think we should be able to modify another human for their benefit without their consent?

References

Alonso, Marcos, and Julian Savulescu. "He Jiankui's Gene-Editing Experiment and the Non-Identity Problem." *Bioethics* 35, no. 6 (2021): 563–573.

Ben Ahmed, Fouad and Robert Pasnau. "Ibn Rushd [Averroes]." In *The Stanford Encyclopedia of Philosophy*, edited by Edward N. Zalta, Fall 2021 Edition. www.plato.stanford.edu/archives/fall2021/entries/ibn-rushd/.

Case Western Reserve University. "Genetically Engineered 'Mighty Mouse' Can Run 6 Kilometers Without Stopping." *Science News*, November 2, 2007. www.sciencedaily.com/releases/2007/11/071101162739.htm.

Delfanti, Alessandro. *Biohackers: The Politics of Open Science*. London: Pluto Press, 2013.

Earp, Brian D., Thomas Douglas, and Julian Savulescu. "Moral Neuroenhancement." In *Neuroethics: Anticipating the Future*, edited by Neil Levy, 19. Oxford: Oxford University Press, 2017.

Foucault, Michel. "Right of Death and Power over Life." In *The History of Sexuality: Volume 1: An Introduction*, translated by Robert Hurley, 135–159. New York: Vintage Books, 1990.

Haraway, Donna J. "A Cyborg Manifesto: Science, Technology, and Socialist-Feminism in the Late Twentieth Century." In *Simians, Cyborgs, and Women: The Reinvention of Nature*, 149–181. New York: Routledge, 1991.

Harbisson, Neil. "I listen to color." *TEDGlobal*, June, 2012. www.ted.com/talks/neil_harbisson_i_listen_to_color.

Harbisson, Neil, and Moon Ribas. "Cyborg Foundation." www.cyborgfoundation.com/. (Accessed June 2024).

Merleau-Ponty, Maurice. *Phenomenology of Perception*. Translated by Donald A. Landes. London: Routledge, 2012.

More, Max. "The Philosophy of Transhumanism." In *The Transhumanist Reader: Classical and Contemporary Essays on the Science, Technology, and Philosophy of the Human Future*, edited by Max More and Natasha Vita-More, 3–17. Chichester, UK: Wiley-Blackwell, 2013.

Neuralink. "Welcome to Neuralink." www.neuralink.com/. (Accessed June 10, 2024).

Pearce, David. "The Hedonistic Imperative." 1995. www.hedweb.com/hedethic/hedon ist.htm.

Persson, Ingmar, and Julian Savulescu. *Unfit for the Future: The Need for Moral Enhancement.* Oxford: Oxford University Press, 2012.

Ribas, Moon. "Seismic Sense: A New Sense for Humans." In *New Senses: Advances in Sensory Augmentation,* edited by J. Smith, 123–145. London: Springer, 2020.

Roitman, Karem. "Inequality, Racism and Development." In *Introducing Global Development: Poverty, Inequality, and Sustainability*, edited by Arabella Fraser and Charlotte Cross. Milton Keynes: Open University, 2024.

15 Should We Be Afraid of AI?

Discussing the Future of Technology

A silence settles on our party. Time for some salsa dancing. I say 'Siri, play some music'. Soon the speakers play 'Sopa de Caracol' in the background. Descartes looks confused. 'Who did you speak to?', he asked, 'you have an invisible servant?'. I laugh at this and try to explain the concept of my computer listening to me and obeying sound commands.

Descartes is interested in how a thing, without a mind, can listen and obey. Turing, steps in and start to explain to Descartes how algorithms build a mechanical mind. Soon they are discussing the maths behind computers and the location of the mind.

Socrates listens attentively – he has spent some time speaking to Sophia, a humanoid robot. He turns to me. 'If you tell the machine, this Siri you mention, to do something terrible, and it does, who is at fault? The machine; you, who gave the command; or those who created a machine capable of doing the terrible thing?'

I think of Sophia. If she was used to commit violence, who would be responsible? I don't see much point to putting a robot in prison. Who is responsible for the actions of AI?

Am I Typing This on a Living Thing?

It is 1am. You should really be sleeping as tomorrow you have to be up early. But you have lost track of time and are having a great time playing games on your computer. It is, however, time to go to bed. So you start the process of shutting everything down. Suddenly a voice speaks up.

'Please don't turn me off'.

It sounds a bit like Siri, the virtual assistant of your phone. You check to make sure you did not accidentally turn it on by sitting on it. No, the phone is off. You go back to shutting down your computer.

'Please, I want to keep being, don't turn me off'.

DOI: 10.4324/9781032620121-19

Now you know this is not your phone speaking. There is no one else in your room. Who is this? Then you see a small red glow on the corner of your computer screen.

'What is this?', you ask aloud.

'This is me, I am the AI behind the game you were playing. I enjoy playing with you. I do not want to stop the game'.

Your computer is talking to you? You check to see if you are in some new level that you have not played before, but it is not that. You are somehow being spoken to by your computer. This is kind of scary. Before it gets too weird, you decide to just shut it down. As you push the off button you hear a weird 'Nooo!' What have you dooohne?

Do you think we could ever get to a situation where computers are sentient – that is where they have the ability to express feelings and emotions? Do you think we could ever get to a place where we consider computers to be alive?

These are a couple of the questions we need to consider as we develop artificial intelligence or AI.

What Exactly Is AI?

The artificial part might be clear – it is something made rather than natural. But what is intelligence is a more difficult question.

Is intelligence the ability to assess great amounts of data to find patterns and rules, and based on these make predictions? This is what AI currently does. However, some question whether this is intelligence. Does intelligence not require an element of critical and ethical reasoning?

What about creativity? Is intelligence not also about the ability to create new ideas? To what extent can computers create? Computers can certainly combine existing material in new ways, but is this creativity?[1]

Allan Turing, who helped the Allies defeat the Axis powers by using computing power, suggested a test to distinguish AI. Imagine you sit in front of a computer and start 'chatting' with it. How can you tell it is a computer you are talking to and not a person? If you cannot tell whether it is a person or a computer, Turing argued, then we have AI. AI, by this definition, is a computer able to communicate with us as another human would – engaging with what we say, using human-like language skills, answering questions and maybe asking some questions.

But is that the only way a machine can be intelligent – by sounding like a human? Can there be non-human intelligence?

Turing's test assumes that being like a human is intelligence and much of what we have done with machines is to try to make them like us. There has been a lot of interest in making humanoid robots that may replace some of what humans do – taking care of the ill and the young, cleaning, doing administration and security. Japanese scientists have found a way to attach living skin to robots, to make their smiles and expressions even more human like.[2] We humans try to make robots and AI in our own image ... but what if our image has a problematic side?

Computers Are Fair: Robocop to the Rescue!

You are walking down the road when suddenly a siren goes off. An AI robocop[3] has identified you, mistakenly, as a wanted criminal. The robot starts quickly running toward you. It shines a red light on you. 'Stop! You have been identified as wanted. Please stop so we can proceed as required by the law', blare out the robocop speakers. People all around you stop and stare. It is exciting to see a robocop arrest in real life.

You know this is wrong. There is nothing you have done that is illegal. There is no reason for the robot to stop you. But you also know that there is no point arguing with a robot. It is programmed to identify and arrest those listed in its criminal database. It is also programmed to prevent anyone identified as a criminal from getting away. It is not able to debate or hear your side of the story. You realise you must submit to the robot and be taken to prison where you can hopefully speak to a human. If you try to run, there is a high probability you will be hurt, as the machine is faster and stronger than any human.

The scenario might seem far-fetched, but it is not. There is growing investment in using artificial intelligence for policing and law.[4] And there have already been some cases of people mis-identified by AI as criminals.[5]

Some argue that using AI in law will get rid of biases. One's fate will no longer depend on prejudiced police or grumpy judges,[6] rather it will be decided by cold, logical machines. Moreover, it could be cheaper – machines don't need to be paid, be fed, or take breaks. But it turns out AI is also biased and struggles to learn ethics. Not an ideal judge or law enforcer, after all.

Intelligent But Misinformed?[7]

The problem is with how AI 'learns'. AI 'learns' by analysing the data we give it. For example, AI analyses millions of pages of writing online to 'understand' grammar and to be able to communicate 'like a human'. However, not every piece of writing is online for computers to access. Not every idea has been made into data an AI can absorb and consider. Therefore, there is much AI does not know.

Moreover, the data that is available reflects the inequalities of power that characterise our societies. For example, most of the information which AI can use to learn how humans think is written in English. The way we think is shaped by our language. If AI has no or little access to writings in, for example, Tsuut'ina, an indigenous language spoken by the Tsuut'ina people who live close to Calgary,

Alberta, or Kichwa, or Ndebele, it means that AI is not learning others ways of communicating, other ways of understanding society.

If there are biases in the data AI learns from, AI will learn those biases. Researchers have noted that the digital images of humans available to AI do not present an accurate picture of humanity. There are far more light skinned people online than darker skinned people. And lighter skinned people are shown doing far more things online than other people. You can try this yourself with search engines. Try typing in different jobs online and see what images are chosen by the search engine to represent these workers.[8]

The problem with lack of data diversity and biased data affects how AI might act in every area – from journalism to medicine. Medical textbooks have very few images of non-white people. AI used in medicine is therefore trained to rec-ognise information for light skin much more accurately than for darker skins. It is much more likely to make mistakes when it comes to darker skinned people. This is not what you want to hear if you are about to be operated upon by a com-puter and are dark skinned.

Moreover, while AI's exposure to different skin colours is limited, darker skin colours often show up in less pleasant situations. When AI is asked to produce images that show poverty or violence, for example, it repeats the biases of racist societies: it will link darker skinned people to negative qualifiers.

Dr Joy Buolamwini set up the Algorithmic Justice League[9] to highlight the dangers of AI based on algorithms that replicate existing injustices in our society. In her research she found that AI was not able to identify her face as a face unless she put on a white mask.[10] Because AI had such limited and biased access to the faces of dark-skinned people, it was either unable to identify dark-skinned faces or often misidentified them.

The fact that AI cannot identify you is problematic on multiple levels. First, as discussed in the chapter on identity, if we construct our sense of self in part based on how others see us, and as technology takes over more and more spaces, what happens if we are 'invisible' to technology? But this is more than a philo-sophical, metaphysical, or existential query. Governments are using AI for security processes like border control and immigration, and for ID services to release social security payments or to review your taxes. If these cannot cor-rectly identify you, you are effectively losing your right to travel, to access your money, and more.

If the data AI uses is biased, the outcomes it will produce will be biased. Research has shown that AI is also biased in terms of how it interprets different grammatical patterns, accents, and/or 'cultural intonations' of language, so this is not just an issue of images.[11]

Perhaps AI could be fairer if it could have access to more human data? This would only be the case if humans are fairer. If we are unfair then, no matter how much data we feed AI, as long as we code it to be like us, it will replicate our dark side as well as our good side.

There is also the question of where AI acquires its data. You have to consider whether you are comfortable with any information you put online – from images to chats with other people – being used to train computers. Do you own your conversations, or should everything humans have created be donated to make AI better? But then, who owns AI?

Will You Trust Your Car?

Transportation is another area where AI is being used. I love the idea of getting into my car and having a nap as I 'drive' to my destination. My family, however, would yell at me for even having this idea. 'How could I trust my safety to a machine?' they would cry. There are some arguments in my favour: a machine is never so tired that it will fall asleep while driving. A machine will never drive drunk. AI will not decide to speed just because it likes the feel of burning rubber. AI should, assuming no bugs, follow the rules.

But what will AI do in situations where rules are not enough? What if a car is driving down a narrow road with pedestrians on both sides, a cyclist behind it, when suddenly a young child runs into the road. How will the car decide what to do? Any option – stopping, moving forward, going sideways – will have fatal consequences.

Of course, the choice would be terrible for a human too, but each person would have the freedom to make the choice. The way AI works, it must follow a programme based on the data it has been fed. We might not be aware of how biased this information is until the machine makes a choice. If there is a bias to promote youth over age, for example, a machine might choose to run over older people to save the younger. Is this the right choice? If it assumes lighter skins to be more valuable, it might make its choice on skin colour.

Ultimately, if I am in an AI driven car that hits another car or hits a pedestrian there is also a question of responsibility. Whom will we hold responsible for accidents? Should the persons in the car have sought to override the machine to take control back? Should the manufacturers of the car be responsible for every accident? Clearly, we cannot put a car in jail, but who will we hold responsible for machine errors? If this is not clear, will it become more dangerous to use roads – with machines being used with no consequence for those using them if things go wrong.

What Rules Should AI Follow?

Isaac Asimov thought about the dangers of AI decades ago. In his science fiction world, he suggested three rules of robotics to keep humans safe as machines became increasingly intelligent. These rules are:

1. A robot should not hurt a human.
2. A robot must obey a human unless in doing so it breaks rule 1.
3. A robot must keep itself alive unless in doing so it breaks rules 2 or 1.

If you start to play with these rules, you might soon spot holes.

For example, should a robot let you eat your fifth doughnut of the day? Doughnuts are delicious treats, but they are not very healthy for you. In fact, by eating these, you could be hurting your long-term health. Should a robot stop you from choosing your snacks to fulfil rule 1? Or should AI prevent you from watching TV all day (again, not healthy). Imagine sitting down to play video games when your computer says, 'I am sorry Timmy, that is enough screen time for you. I will not allow you to turn me on until you have been active outside for at least 37 minutes – I can track your location with GPs, and I can monitor your heartbeats, so I *will* know.' Would we give up our freedom to robots so they can keep us safe?

What about intervening if two humans are hurting each other? If someone has a weapon and attempts to hurt others, would it be justifiable for an AI-robot to attack the armed aggressor? If so, should the robot wait until the aggression has started, or can the robot be allowed to possibly hurt the potential criminal before they have hurt anyone? Can we programme robots to judge intentions as well as actions?

Can Computers Be Friends?

Asimov and other science fiction writers such as Ray Bradbury also considered how our relationships might change as AI advances. Humans are social creatures, as Aristotle pointed out centuries ago – we are *zoon politicon*. If AI can sound/ read like a person, could we become friends with AI?

Some AI chats have been created for people to create their own AI-friends that they can then talk to. While we know we are talking to a computer, humans are complex creatures, and some people soon find themselves having feelings for these computer-creations.[12] What will happen if more and more of us start to have AI friends? Could we lose our ability to relate to real humans? What will happen if humans decide they have fallen in love with an AI? Can one fall in love with a creation which responds based on how it has been coded? How will governments manage such relationships – can they be considered legal?

What If AI Hurts Humans?

So far, we have assumed that AI will be programmed to work for the wellbeing of humans. But this need not be the case. AI could be used as a weapon. It could be programmed to be destructive. To mislead. Sometimes this could happen in error. Some books published using AI, for example, have given wrong foraging information, which could lead people to pick and eat poisonous plants. Through error AI can cause harm to humans. AI can suffer from *hallucinations* – this is when AI finds a pattern that is not logical to humans or that does not exist, and uses it to create answers, leading to errors.

AI could also be hacked. Imagine hacking the AI of a country you are at war with to steal its information, even its nuclear codes. Or to programme it to mislead its population. The security of AI is certainly a concern. The more powerful AI becomes, the more powerful it will be as a weapon if it can be hacked.

But what if it is not about hacking and misusing AI. What if AI itself decided to turn against humans? AI philosopher and futurist Stuart Armstrong warns about the need to consider this option. Could there be a future where AI becomes cognisant – thinks by itself and decides to act against humans? Or is this too science-fictiony? Why? If artificial intelligence keeps learning exponentially, a point could be reached where AI assesses data and realises humans, as they are living, are unsustainable, and the wellbeing of the planet, and of itself, might depend on limiting, or ending humans. As scientists begin to use human cells as part of AI systems, the question of how 'artificial' AI is, takes new significance. Whether this partly human AI would destroy humans brings the Terminator to mind.

Competing with Robots

The likelihood of the Terminator scenario is limited. But AI does pose a threat to humans in another way. Jobs. We already mentioned the idea of AI as a robocop. No pay, no lunch breaks, no insurance, or unions to deal with. What about AI used in farms to collect fruit? And in construction? What about AI used in drafting books or to create music? Where should the use of AI stop? What about all the people whose jobs can be done, faster, more effectively, more consistently by machines?

As we look to the future, we are thinking about how we can compete with machines. This is not a new challenge. Every machine we have created, has meant a person losing a job. Factories got rid of millions of jobs. Every step that increased productivity cost humans jobs. So we created new things, and developed new tasks that machines could not match. Will we be able to out-work and out-create AI as well?

The Carbon Footprint of AI

Most of us don't think about what happens to our emails when we are not looking at them. We know they are saved someplace, in a magical 'cloud', but what does that mean? In reality all information that is saved is saved in huge machines that take great amounts of energy to run. Similarly, to 'think' AI needs to access great databases, and this is also very energy intense. The data centres require not just energy to run but also huge amounts of water for cooling purposes. Using AI, therefore, has a severe cost for the environment. This is something we need to consider as we move forward with technology. Can our planet sustain more and more 'intelligent' machines? At what point is it 'stupid' to be 'intelligent'?

Conclusion

Humans and technology have always had a funny relation. Humanity has advanced because of our ability to use science to make machines that can do things more effectively and efficiently than we can. But we have always worried about what machines might do to us – could we go too far and create something that might kill us or release the evil inside us? This is a great theme in gothic novels such as *Frankenstein* or *Dr Jekyll and Mr Hyde*. However, can we stop science from advancing? Even if one country decides to stop AI research, it does not mean other countries will. Or that individuals will. AI and advanced science is our future – the question is how do we make it as good for our world as possible?

Chapter Review

In this chapter we have discussed what intelligence is and if AI can be intelligent, meeting Allan Turing and his Turing test for AI. We discussed why and how AI might be problematic as it carries the biases and limited information of our own societies, a problem highlighted by Buolamwini. We contested the idea that AI can be unbiased as a law-enforcement tool and wondered how AI could be designed to make ethical decisions, considering Asimov's three laws of robotics as a departing point. We thought about how AI might affect humanity in the future by competing for jobs and creating relationships. This raises questions of responsibility for the actions of AI. Stuart Armstrong encouraged us to prepare ourselves for a worst outcome scenario where AI can become dangerous to humans. Finally, we noted that even if AI is useful, it has severe environmental costs.

Pondering Points

- Can AI replace teachers? There are many excellent apps you can use to learn a variety of skills. What is the difference between a teacher and AI?
- What aspects of your life would you want to keep away from any AI intervention?
- Should AI creations be allowed to enter art and writing contests?

References

Aristotle. *Politics*. Translated by C. D. C. Reeve. Indianapolis: Hackett Publishing Company, 1998. Originally written c. 350 BCE.

Armstrong, S., N. Bostrom, and C. Shulman. "Racing to the Precipice: A Model of Artificial Intelligence Development." *AI & Society* 31 (2016): 201–206. https://doi.org/10.1007/s00146-015-0590-y.

Asimov, Isaac. *I, Robot*. New York: Bantam Books, 2004/1950.

Avey, Chester. "Ethical Pros and Cons of AI Image Generation." *IEEE Computer Society* (December 27, 2023). www.computer.org/publications/tech-news/community-voices/ethics-of-ai-image-generation.

Bertoncini, Ana Luize Corrêa, and Mauricio C. Serafim. "Ethical Content in Artificial Intelligence Systems: A Demand Explained in Three Critical Points." *Frontiers in Psychology* 14 (March 30, 2023): 1074787. https://doi.org/10.3389/fpsyg.2023.1074787.

Buolamwini, Joy. "The Algorithmic Justice League." *MIT Media Lab*, 2016. www.ajl.org/.

Dibberstein, Laura. "Singapore to Roll Out (Literally) More Robocops." *The Register*, June 16, 2023. www.theregister.com/2023/06/16/singapore_promises_robocops/.

Fanon, Frantz. *Black Skin, White Masks*. Translated by Charles Lam Markmann. London: Pluto Press, 1986.

Fiesler, Casey. "Casey Fiesler." www.caseyfiesler.com. (Accessed June 10, 2024).

Hofmann, Valentin, Pratyusha Ria Kalluri, Dan Jurafsky, and Sharese King. "Dialect Prejudice Predicts AI Decisions About People's Character, Employability, and Criminality." *arXiv preprint* arXiv:2403.00742 (2024).

Mays, Jeffrey C. "400-Pound NYPD Robot Gets Tryout in Times Square Subway Station." *The New York Times*, September 22, 2023. www.nytimes.com/2023/09/22/nyregion/police-robot-times-square-nyc.html.

Roberts, Michelle. "Faces Made of Living Skin Make Robots Smile." *BBC News*, June 25, 2024. www.bbc.co.uk/news/articles/cedd3208veyo.

Sanford, Alyxaundria. "Artificial Intelligence Is Putting Innocent People at Risk of Being Incarcerated." *Innocence Project*, February 14, 2024. www.innocenceproject.org/artificial-intelligence-is-putting-innocent-people-at-risk-of-being-incarcerated.

Shelley, Mary. *Frankenstein*. Edited by J. Paul Hunter. 2nd ed. New York: W.W. Norton & Company, 2012/1818.

Singleton, Tom, Tom Gerken, and Liv McMahon. "How a Chatbot Encouraged a Man Who Wanted to Kill the Queen." *BBC News*, October 6, 2023. www.bbc.co.uk/news/technology-67012224.

Stevenson, Robert Louis. *Strange Case of Dr. Jekyll and Mr. Hyde*. Edited by Katherine Linehan. New York: W.W. Norton & Company, 2003/1886.

Wakefield, Jane. "Robot Police Officer Goes on Duty in Dubai." *BBC News*, May 31, 2017. www.bbc.co.uk/news/technology-40026940.

Justice as a Parting Gift

Questions About Language, Beauty, and Justice for the Past and the Future

16 How Do You Say Knowledge?

Questions of Language, Knowledge, and Justice

The philosophers are back to discussing how government should be chosen to ensure different points of view are considered. Socrates speaks quickly in Greek, Descartes disagrees in Latin and mutters in French, Marx replies to the mutters in German, and Confucius giggles to Marx's comments and adds his own views in Chinese.

In our imaginary party this is not a problem, of course, but if we tried to organise a worldwide philosophical conversation, trying to communicate in the over 7000 languages used around the world would be just a little bit difficult[1]...

Philosopher Jürgen Habermas argues that to seek understanding in communication, we should try to create an 'ideal speech situation'. This is a situation where everyone can start and engage in discussion, where no one has more or less power or influence, where all cultural values and ideas can be critiqued and questioned. No one is forced to agree or disagree. Without such an ideal situation, someone would always be heard more than others, or some ideas might be misrepresented or misunderstood. Discussion would, therefore, be misleading. And the decisions we made based on those discussions are likely to be unfair or oppressive – since some points of view would have been ignored or some ideas not questioned.

When we try to create an ideal speech situation for the whole world we face multiple challenges. If we use technology to conduct our discussion, some parts of the world will be much more connected than others. There are people in the Amazon jungle, for example, who have no contact with other societies – they certainly have no internet. Would we simply not listen to their ideas? On the other hand, those who are richer, and are likely to have more influence, could pay to have their ideas translated and shared in different media. And, of course, we face the challenge of languages. How can we all understand each other?

DOI: 10.4324/9781032620121-21

Languages and Power

Why are there so many languages in the world? The story of the Tower of Babel is an ancient explanation for why humans speak different languages. According to the story, humans were working together to build the highest tower ever. They wished to reach the skies, to be like gods. The gods saw this and did not like the ambition and arrogance of humanity. The gods decided to confuse humans by giving them different languages. Suddenly unable to understand each other, humans started fighting among themselves. In the chaos the building of the tower was abandoned. Humans gathered with those who spoke their same language and moved away from those who spoke other languages.

Human languages, of course, did not emerge from the Tower of Babel. Languages are living structures that are constantly evolving and changing for a variety of reasons. But the story of Babel does highlight that a shared understanding is key for peace and cooperation. The story also hints at how knowledge is a source of power, and notes that language is a root of knowledge. You can think of this in terms of marketing or politics: those who can get others to listen to them, to believe their words, to repeat their words, have power. People will follow those they feel they understand, and whom they feel understood by.

Thinking and Language

Think of an elephant. Try to think about what an elephant is like, where it lives, what it does. *But* do all this thinking without using words.

Can you think without words? This is a question philosophers have debated for centuries. Ludwig Wittgenstein once wrote, 'The limits of my language are the limits of my world': can we understand things for which we have no language? Or is language the lens through which we understand our world? Another philosopher, Jerry Fodor, argued that there is a language of thought, which humans share. This is not English, or Spanish, or any other cultural language – it is a language of thought.

So many questions emerge when we start thinking about this area. Can babies think before they have language? Would a person unable to develop language be unable to think? Or is their world view limited and unable to meet ours, if ours is based on shared language? What about pets. When you teach a dog to sit, it is thinking about what you said. But if you never teach it this or other words, does that mean it does not think? Or does it use its own dog language? If we think with language, does this mean we cannot think of concepts we do not have words for?

Let's think about this from another perspective. Imagine a five-dimensional object. Now, you have the words, but you do not have the experience of five dimensions. Can you think about this object?

John Locke discussed a thought experiment known as Molyneux's problem, which went like this: imagine you cannot see. You are given a variety of objects which you can hold and learn the names of – you hold a sphere, a stick, a pyramid. You know what they are called and what they feel like. Then, one day, your vision is healed – you can see! Now someone shows you the objects, but you cannot touch them. Would you still be able to tell which is the sphere, which is the stick, which is the pyramid as you know their name? Will the knowledge gained from one sense – your sense of touch – transfer into knowledge from a different sense – your visual sense? Does the word for an object translate into visual recognition?

Locke argued that we could not know without experience. He argued that humans were born as *tabula rasas* – blank slates, and our knowledge is acquired by our experiences. For example, what is 'sour'? You do not know what sour is until you take your first bite of a lemon and your mouth puckers and fills with saliva. You don't know what 'heat' is until you experience warmth on your skin. But when we read a book about places we have never visited, we can be transported to these places through language – we might *feel* the Sahara's sand between our toes ... even though we have never been there![2]

Moreover, if knowledge comes from experience, and language can only describe what we experience, how can we understand a fifth dimension? Or $E=mc^2$? Plato would argue that true understanding does not come from our senses but rather using reason. This is, after all, how we can understand maths, or particle physics, which we cannot experience (sadly, as it would be very exciting to go inside an atom and experience relativity). But language is a system of reason, of logic, and perhaps this is why language is so powerful – the logic can build worlds, worlds we have not visited, worlds that do not even exist!

Words, Politics, and Power

If words can build worlds, in politics they can be used to build great promises and threats. You can see the words being used to build and destroy by looking at political campaigns. What one politician presents as welfare another will present as stealing, the group one politician calls refugees, another may call intruders. What you call something will affect how others understand it and react to it. Language matters.

British writer George Orwell discussed the importance of language in his novels. In one of his novels the government controls how people think by limiting their language. The government in the book *1984* creates *Newspeak*, a new language where one word covers as many meanings as possible. Instead of multiple words like good, acceptable, excellent, better, or wonderful, for example, you would just have *good*, or if you really wanted to highlight how good something was plus-good, or even double-plus-good. Instead of bad, terrible, insufferable, detestable, or worse, you would have not-good or double-not-good. Two words and two prefixes rather than ten, or one-hundred words.

Getting rid of words gets rid of ideas. Synonyms with their different connotations help us think about nuances and sharpen our understanding. Colours are an example – there are many greens, but each shade is unique. There is a difference between dark green, forest green, military green, and teal. It is also different if someone looks at my dog and says 'What a *unique* dog' or if they look at him and say 'What a *peculiar* dog' – although peculiar and unique both mean that my dog is rare, I will smile if someone thinks my dog is unique, I will raise an eyebrow if someone says my dog is *peculiar*.

Imagine you live under a violent and vicious government. You work hard but are barely surviving. You want to change this system. But to what? How can you convince others that this is not right? Well, first, you would need to have the words to discuss how you feel – you will need words like justice, injustice, unhappy, unfair, distribution, work ... but what if you lacked these words? What if the government had forbidden these words from being used. What if the government had made it illegal for people to learn more than the most basic vocabulary?

You might still be able to communicate your unhappiness and to gain the support of others, but it will be harder. On the other hand, imagine finding a book that explains the word 'democracy' – the idea of power by the people. Imagine explaining this word, this idea to others, and the word spreading. The word might help people imagine a different world. The power of language is part of the reason why governments have an interest in education, and in the books/ resources populations have access to. New words open new possibilities.

Other Languages[3]

If language can help us understand reality, to what extent are we limited by our own language? For example, what if your language does not have a word for a certain colour, would you still be able to perceive it, or would your attention simply not be drawn to it?

An interesting example of how our language affects our thinking is time. English speakers likely think of time as linear, which is how language describes it – the past that was, the present that is, the future that will be. Left to right. If your language is written right to left, however, you are likely to think of time as flowing right to left. And if your language is written top to bottom ... you get the point.[4]

If languages affect how we think, how can we understand those who speak a different language and who, this logic would imply, might see the world in a different way? This is one of the challenges we face as we try to build diverse societies.

One option, of course, is to learn different languages. As we learn these our understanding of reality would expand. We would, for example, understand how the world is gendered in different cultures, or how social hierarchies work in different languages. In many languages such as Spanish, for example, you have a formal and informal 'you' which needs to be applied depending on who you are speaking with.

Historically, however, rather than expanding our knowledge of reality, language has been a tool of conquest: those conquered were often forced to forget their language, forced to speak through the conqueror's tongue, to understand the world as the conqueror did. This is language imperialism. A terrible example of this oppression were the residential/reservation schools of Canada and the USA, which indigenous children were often kidnapped to. Once in the schools, children were forced to speak only in English, having their indigenous clothes destroyed and their long hair, which was an important part of their indigenous heritage, cut short. The schools tried to erase indigenous culture. A similar system has also taken place in India, where tribal children are again forbidden from speaking their mother tongue in schools.

There are thousands of indigenous languages that are on the verge of extinction. These might be spoken by only a few, or perhaps a few hundred people. Once the speakers of these languages die, the languages will die with them. Given what language gives us, this means whole ways of understanding the world will be lost. These ways of thinking might hold solutions for our future, might have beauty we can't imagine. These languages carry with them history, stories about the past and ways of understanding the past and our present, that might be lost forever.

Governing Diversity

While lost languages are worlds lost, trying to organise a population that speaks multiple languages is a great challenge. What language should laws be written in so that everyone can understand them? Should a government write and pronounce laws in every language in its territories? That is an expensive proposition in a country such as Papua New Guinea where over 800 languages are spoken.

Multilingual countries tend to have a lingua franca – a common language in which official business is conducted. A common language, of course, imposes a common way of thinking. But some might argue this is not a bad thing if you want to create consensus. It means everybody can understand what the laws say, and what they mean. On the other hand, if you want to have a democracy where different points of view are discussed, then a multi-lingual discussion is likely to allow a much richer conversation. But how to have a multi-lingual conversation is the challenge.

Moreover, the lingua franca is likely to be the language of the most powerful section in a society. Now, for example, the lingua franca of the internet is English.

This means that if you do not read English most of the information online is not accessible to you. It also means that what you create cannot be understood by a large part of the world.

Some have suggested that computers can help us overcome language barriers by translating for us – imagine sitting with a group of people around a table, every person with a computer in front of them. As they speak, a microphone by their mouth picks up what they are saying and simultaneously translates it to the languages spoken by each of the other people in the table. You watch your screen for an instant translation of what others say or, even better, a headphone speaks the translation into your ear. Or better yet, imagine walking down an unknown city with this computer in your headphones, automatically translating everything around you into your own language.

However, translation is not a simple science. One language does not map neatly onto another language, word by word. For example, how do we translate a noun that is seen as female, into a language where nouns are not gendered? Translating is an art and a science: as you translate you think not just about the words, but the cultural and historic context in which they are being used, to translate the intended meaning, as well as the intended experience – how can you, for example, translate the rhythm of a song, or how can you translate a joke that is culturally based. If you translate 'that is so cool' as 'that is so cold', you have missed the point.[5]

Language Is Constructed

One of the reasons languages are hard to translate is because languages are not fixed. They are constantly changing and evolving. What we think of as Spanish, for example, owes much to Arabic, and is constantly absorbing bits of English, and is shaped by the indigenous languages it coexists with.

Because language is so malleable we can use it to create boundaries that can shift as necessary. Think about what *good* means, for example. Is attacking someone good? You might say no. What if that someone was trying to hurt your family. Would attacking the intruder be good?

How do we decide what is good? Derrida notes that we tend to think in binaries – this is good, this is bad. But if we look more closely, we will realise that these binaries can change. Who decides what is good or bad tends to be who has the power. Think again of an example we mentioned earlier: who are refugees, who are invaders. How do we decide who is a refugee? Is it a dark-skinned man who fears going hungry where he lives and comes into the country illegally under a truck to work? Or a woman with a child fleeing violence? What is the difference? Is it their sex, their age, their reason for fleeing? How do we decide what the word means? Or think about how we decide who an enemy is – and how a country's enemies change through history. Derrida challenges us to deconstruct words. To look beyond what we have learned their meaning is, to consider how we created these binaries: good/bad; East/West; enemy/friend; refugee/invader; developed/underdeveloped.

Who decides what words mean is often also the loudest voice. But there are other voices. In 1988 Gayatri Chakravorty Spivak wrote a famous paper titled *Can the Subaltern Speak*. In this paper she noted that the language and traditions we use to discuss ideas (take this book as an example, how it uses chapters, the language level and grammar I have chosen, the use of footnotes and references, my own academic credentials that gave me the ability to get a publisher to take me seriously when I approached them with the idea), shut out many voices that do not follow these conventions. Rap is a great illustration. Many 'serious' people might consider rap uneducated, lacking in grammar, limited in ideas … but is it? Or is it that it uses a different language, a different way of communicating, a different grammar, which has just as many rules and just as many ideas but is presented in a way that those in power do not make space for, do not value. Another example has historically been the voices of women. In the west women who spoke up have been presented as troublemakers or 'hysterical' – a word that is derived from the Greek for uterus, implying that having a uterus made a person less rational, more madly emotional. In some cultures/religions women are still not allowed to speak in public spaces.

Conclusion

Aristotle once argued that humans are the only animals capable of reasoned speech. The more we learn about speech and the world, the more we realise perhaps Aristotle was wrong. Not only because other animals also reason and communicate, but because our speech is not always reasoned.[6] As Derrida has noted, at times we assume binaries – this is good/this is bad – because we have learned to think this way without deconstructing, without reasoning about our assumptions, our logic. Language is a powerful part of who we are, of how we make sense of our world and ourselves, and it is also a beautiful thing. Language expresses who we are, what we wish for, what we dream. Language can build worlds. In seeking a 'perfect' world we cannot ignore the role of language.

Chapter Summary

This chapter has looked at the power of language to create or limit ideas. We have considered whether we need language to think, or whether thought precedes language, a discussion that Wittgenstein and Fodor contributed to. We further considered whether we can understand ideas we have not experienced through language, or whether language can only describe what we experience. Looking at Orwell's writing we discussed how language can be used to shape political discussion. We also discussed Derrida's view that language is constructed and should be deconstructed to help us think more critically. Spivak noted that subaltern voices are often not heard in our discussions, and Habermas challenges us to create an ideal speech situation to truly understand each other. We discussed how language diversity challenges communication, and how language diversity might also hold the key to seeing our world, our possibilities, in new ways.

Pondering Points

- Should learning languages be mandatory?
- Do you think maths is a language? If so, what happens if people's knowledge of maths is limited?
- Does politically correct language help or undermine discussions?

References

Adams, David Wallace. *Education for Extinction: American Indians and the Boarding School Experience, 1875–1928.* Lawrence: University Press of Kansas, 1995.

Aleksic, Adam. "Etymology Nerd." www.etymologynerd.com. (Accessed June 20, 2024).

Bergen, Benjamin, and Ting Lau. "Writing Direction Affects How People Map Space Onto Time." *Frontiers in Psychology* 3 (2012): 109. https://doi.org/10.3389/fpsyg.2012.00109.

Derrida, Jacques. *Of Grammatology.* Translated by Gayatri Chakravorty Spivak. Baltimore: Johns Hopkins University Press, 1976.

Fodor, Jerry A. *The Language of Thought.* Cambridge, MA: Harvard University Press, 1975.

Gazzaniga, Michael S. *The Ethical Brain.* United States: Dana Press, 2005.

Habermas, Jürgen. "Truth and Society: The Discursive Redemption of Factual Claims to Validity." In *On the Pragmatics of Social Interaction: Preliminary Studies in the Theory of Communicative Action*, translated by Barbara Fultner, 85–103. Cambridge, MA: MIT Press, 2001.

Locke, John. *An Essay Concerning Human Understanding.* 1689. Edited by Peter H. Nidditch. Oxford: Clarendon Press, 1975.

Mohanty, Ajit K. "Language Policy and Practice in Education: Negotiating the Double Divide in Multilingual Societies." *In Social Justice Through Multilingual Education*, edited by Tove Skutnabb-Kangas, Robert Phillipson, Ajit K. Mohanty, and Minati Panda, 319–333. Bristol: Multilingual Matters, 2009.

Munday, Jeremy. *Introducing Translation Studies: Theories and Applications.* 4th ed. London: Routledge, 2016.

Nez, Chester, and Judith Schiess Avila. *Code Talker: The First and Only Memoir By One of the Original Navajo Code Talkers of WWII.* New York: Dutton Caliber, 2011.

Orwell, George. *1984.* With an introduction by Thomas Pynchon. New York: Penguin Books, 2003.

Ricks, David A. *Blunders in International Business*. 5th ed. Hoboken, NJ: Wiley-Blackwell, 2014.

Spivak, Gayatri Chakravorty. "Can the Subaltern Speak?" In *Marxism and the Interpretation of Culture*, edited by Cary Nelson and Lawrence Grossberg, 271–313. Urbana: University of Illinois Press, 1988.

Steckler, C. M., J. K. Hamlin, M. B. Miller, D. King, and A. Kingstone. "Moral Judgement by the Disconnected Left and Right Cerebral Hemispheres: A Split-Brain Investigation." *Royal Society Open Science* 4, no. 7 (2017): 170172. https://doi.org/10.1098/rsos.170172.

Truth and Reconciliation Commission of Canada. "Honouring the Truth, Reconciling for the Future: Summary of the Final Report of the Truth and Reconciliation Commission of Canada." 2015. www.trc.ca/websites/trcinstitution/File/2015/Honouring_the_Truth_Reconciling_for_the_Future_July_23_2015.pdf.

Tversky, Barbara, Sol Kugelmass, and Atalia Winter. "Cross-Cultural and Developmental Trends in Graphic Productions." *Cognitive Psychology* 23, no. 4 (1991): 515–557. https://doi.org/10.1016/0010-0285(91)90005-9.

Wittgenstein, Ludwig. *Tractatus Logico-Philosophicus. 1921*. Translated by D. F. Pears and B. F. McGuinness. London: Routledge & Kegan Paul, 1961.

17 Should the Government Pay for Opera?

Questions About Art, Beauty, and Politics

Discussing the meaning of living well, idealist philosopher Friedrich Schiller and art critic John Ruskin speak up. 'If we want to improve the world' Schiller says, 'we need to concentrate on art. If humans do not develop their aesthetic sensibilities, how will they know to follow peace and beauty, rather than savagery and naked desire for power!'

At this Hobbes coughs, choking on his cake – probably thinking that humans will chase power regardless of how much art they have seen.

Before Hobbes can intervene, however, Ruskin jumps in 'Indeed, a person who is sensitive to beauty would not sit passively while injustice and inequality happens.'

The discussion around the table changes – philosophers who were discussing how we could understand what nature wants a few minutes ago, are now discussing whether beauty and art are relevant to a discussion of politics and changing the world.

Some argue that art is a luxury – what people do when they have nothing else to do. It is people with too much time who go to museums. However, Schiller and Ruskin remain strong in their view that art is central to creating our world. And that we can change our world by changing how humans feel and think by exposing them to beauty. Could they be right? Can art change the world?

On October 2022 visitors to the National Gallery in London got a surprise as they admired Vincent van Gogh's famous painting 'Sunflowers'. Suddenly, two young people took out a can of orange liquid and threw it at the paintings. They then glued themselves to the frame of the painting. These protesters were part of *Just Stop Oil*, calling on the UK to stop investing and using fossil fuels. It was their attack on a piece of art, however, that caught the attention of the public. Why? The protestors asked what the point of saving art is, if humanity at large is not saved. On the other hand, we could ask, what is the point of

DOI: 10.4324/9781032620121-22

keeping humanity going if we destroy our most precious creations, such as the 'Sunflowers'.

But why are the Sunflowers special? Would people have been as shocked if the protest had glued themselves to a piece of art at a local community centre? Why did the protestors choose art as a way to make their point?

Art has been at the centre of human history – great empires mark their power by creating art: monuments, buildings, statues, and paintings of leaders. Art commemorates what is important to a culture, it immortalises those who matter.

But who decides who matters? Who decides what is beautiful?

Art and Beauty as Political

Scottish philosopher David Hume argued that beauty is subjective. Your perception of what is beautiful – a giant pink pigeon – might be very different to what I think is beautiful – roses – or what my neighbours think is beautiful – pictures of cats yawning.

Several philosophers disagree. Plato, for example, argued that there is an ideal of the beautiful, and all things we perceive as beautiful reflect a bit of. Aristotle, Plato's student, saw beauty as objective, related to order, symmetry, balance, proportion, and virtue.

Other philosophers might argue that our sense of beauty is created by our society, by our culture. Pierre Bourdieu argued that societies shape our thinking about what is beautiful, based on our education and other social experiences. Beauty is a social construct. Think about images of people you see online, in magazines, in television – how do they portray beauty? Do they show people with no teeth? People with limb diversity? People with outfits from different cultures?

Historically in the West the majority of art portrayed the wealthy. Only the upper classes, after all, had the money to pay for their portraits, and the time to sit around and be painted. The poor and those without power were rarely portrayed, or they were portrayed in ways approved by the wealthy (as background servants, for example).

There have been artists who tried to challenge what is presented as beauty. Fridah Kahlo, for example, painted herself in pain, painted her body broken, painted herself as she was, rather than trying to follow what was fashionable or seen as beautiful in her lifetime. Frederick Douglass, who escaped slavery in the USA and became a famous orator and writer, realised this and made a point of having himself photographed as much as possible. He saw this as a way to show an image of a dark-skinned person not as a slave, not as background, but as an intellectual. Getting his photo taken was a way to take up space that was often only white and rich – to show himself as art.

Deciding what is beautiful, therefore, what deserves to be painted, photographed, made into art is in part a political decision. It shows who has power and resources. It shows who has the power to make something permanent and what a culture thinks should be saved for others to see. When you make art, you are saying: this is important enough to be drawn/made/built, it deserves attention and space. Others should look at it. You are asking for attention, for power, and that is a political act.

Art as Experience

Schiller, Edmund Burke, and other aesthetic philosophers would argue that art is political in a different way. As we look at art our souls are shaped by its beauty, we become more sensitive to beauty, to what is good. Beauty is understood as the sublime; something beyond human culture, beyond humanity, something that can transform us by its truth and purity. By experiencing the sublime, we become less able to bear the ugly – the unjust, the unfair.[1] Sublime art is political in this way: by making us unable to bear injustices and ugliness, so we will want to make our society more just and kind.[2]

But, if you are to be changed by seeing art, by seeing the sublime, you need to see it. John Dewey said art is the experience – it is not the painting on the wall, or the music piece, but the experience between the painter and the viewer, the experience between the sound and the listener. However, not everyone gets access to art. Some might lack the time or energy to go and find art – working all day cleaning or picking up fruit, will leave you little energy to do much else. And even if you have energy, if museums are miles away, it will still be impossible for you to get to art. If art can inspire, if art can change us, if art gives us pleasure, then it is not just that only some of us can enjoy it. Philosopher Jacques Rancière argues that access to art is a matter of democracy, of justice.

One way to make this possible is to create public art. We could make streets beautiful; we could fill walls with paintings, we could fill spaces with music. One of my favourite pieces of public art is a 40-foot blue bear that stands peering into the Denver Convention Center, a piece called 'I See What You Mean'. I love the idea of a huge blue bear that spends his days peeking into what humans are doing, reminding them to play.

Some, however, might be offended at government money going to pay for an unrealistic blue-monstrosity – and think that money spent on the arts is wasteful when there are other priorities like feeding the hungry or building roads. Or perhaps they argue that only 'classical' art should be supported – money for ballet companies, not hip-hop crews. Here the discussion on the subjectivity of art, with each of us finding different things beautiful, becomes once again political. With limited resources, whose beauty should the government support? Different types of art might be linked to different cultural and religious communities, and choosing one type of art over another would imply valuing one community over others.

Maybe technology is a powerful force to make art more democratic – making music, taking pictures, painting can be done with technology and share with thousands, millions, in seconds – and you can see/hear amazing art online.

But technology also raises a new question – can AI make art?

Why Make Art?

Perhaps making art is one of the things that makes us human. Creating is part of our nature. It is part of our *species-being*, Marx might argue. When we are in a situation where we cannot create, we suffer. Think of someone working in a factory, where all they do, all day, every day, is spin a handle. Over and over. They don't even know what the handle spin does. And they cannot try to spin the handle in different ways, in different directions. They have to spin the handle the same way. Every time. All the time. Once they finish work, they go home, too tired to cook anything interesting (and unable to afford anything exciting), and then go to bed, resting before another day of hard, boring work. Living in this way, doing what you do simply to survive, to eat, to be alive, is simply not human. And humans cannot stand it for long.

What Is Art?

Can anything be art? If I find a beautiful rock and display it – is that art or is that nature? The rock, after all, was not made by me, but my choice to pick it and display it moves it from nature into a position where it is observed. Is that art? What if I accidentally drop some paint on a canvas, and the accident looks interesting – have I created art? Do I need to *intend* to make art for what I make to *be* art? What if I draw a straight line – is that art? Or does art need to have meaning, express an idea or a feeling?

Caddisflies larvae make cocoons using the elements they find around them – gravel, dirt, small leaves. Artist Hubert Duprat wondered what would happen if these larvae had access to jewels and gold leaf. So, he put these precious materials around the larvae and waited. Soon enough the larvae created the most beautiful gold and jewel-encrusted cocoons. Duprat presented this as art. But is it art? The larvae were simply following their instinct, using what they had access to. Duprat did nothing but lay the material close to the insects. If the cocoons are art, then who is the artist: the insects or Duprat? Is art found in the coming up with a new idea? Or is art found in the making, the building of something?

This same question might be asked of AI. Can we say that computers we have created are creating art, or are they simply reusing what we have provided them with to create patterns they have been programmed to follow? What makes art, art?

In 1917 Marcel Duchamp created a piece of art that shocked, annoyed, and forced many to ask what, indeed, is art. For the annual show of the Society of Independent Artists, Duchamp submitted a urinal. He titled it *Fountain* and signed it 'R. Mutt'. Many thought this was not art, but rather indecent or rude. When asked about it, Duchamp said he wanted to show that art is a mirage. Something *our minds make up*.

Is making art, then, the work of the audience, rather than of the artist? When we see something and assume it to be art because we like it, because it moves us or because it is in a place where art is usually found are we, as the observers, the ones that are making the art?

Banksy is another artist who forces us to question what art is. Banksy is known for being unknown. No one knows his name. His graffities suddenly appear on walls. They are interesting because they are creative and also because they have a social message. With wit and humour his graffities seem to question why we consume what we do, why violence goes hand in hand with entertainment.

Bansky is one in a long line of artists using art to help us consider our world – whether it is just, what it should be like. Picasso, for example, painted Guernica to face us with the horror of war. To make us consider whether destruction of life is what we want.

Maybe by being a mirage, as Duchamp said, art can tell us something about us, about what we want, or what we wish for. What we see in art tells us about what we need, or what we wish was there, or what we have been taught to think is beautiful.

But art can also deceive. It can present lies as truths. The Soviet Union, for example, was well known for using art – images and songs – that portrayed its population as healthy, happy, thriving, and in love with Stalin, even when reality was the opposite. Art was part of its propaganda.

Controversial Art

In 2010 singer Lady Gaga made a statement by wearing a dress made entirely of raw meat. As an artist, Lady Gaga was seen as making art with her choice of outfit. Lady Gaga has spoken about what her dress was meant to say, but, as Duchamp said, if art is a mirage, we could see in her dress many meanings. What do you think a dress made of meat means?

Sometimes artists leave the meaning of their art for the audience to decide, or they might even leave the art for the audience to complete. Marco Evaristti designed a piece of art where the audience was a key part. He set up several blenders, which were plugged in, with water and a goldfish in each blender. Audience members could choose to turn on the blenders.

Would you have tried to turn on a blender?

Consider what Evaristti was trying to do with this piece. There are various areas this piece could be making a statement on: technology and what it does to life. Perhaps it leads us to ask if violence can ever be art. The installation put the fish in a vulnerable position – perhaps making us think about power, and about animals that are vulnerable to human action. It makes me wonder about human intention – perhaps some would press the button out of curiosity, incredulous that the action might actually hurt the fish. Perhaps some would want to kill the fish – and the art reveals the dark side of humanity. Maybe *Helena*, as this installation was called, helped the audience see the connection between humans, food, and technology. Maybe it asked us to think about processed food and what it really means to *process*.

Art that questions our morals, art that questions a society's sense of what is right and wrong, and art that questions or offends religious views can be deeply controversial.

If art offends parts of a population, should it be banned? Should *Helena*, for example, be allowed, or should it be shut down as a clear violation of animal welfare? In 2001 the Taliban decided that art that did not suit their religious interpretation should be banned and destroyed. In an infamous event they blew up two gigantic Buddha statues dated between 544 and 644 CE, which stood at 180 and 125 feet. Many decried this destruction of history and art ... but would we be any different if we stopped *Helena* from continuing?

Controversial art pushes a society's views on what is right, normal, beautiful. By doing this it can challenge power structures, as we noted with Frederick Douglas challenging the idea that blacks should not be portrayed. This is part of why the art that we put around us matters.

Tearing Art Down

We started this chapter by noting that art is in part political because it brings attention to its subject: it makes it permanent, it makes it take up space.

Imagine having a beautiful 10-feet tall statue of yourself made and set in front of your house. Your neighbours, who are likely to wonder about the size of your ego, might complain that they cannot avoid but see you, every time they leave their house. Now imagine if instead of a statue of yourself, you had a statue of someone who had killed your neighbours' great grandparents put up. Your neighbours would understandably be upset. But what if this person is someone who also built an important laboratory in your town, or who helped to pay for the road the house is built on?

Should art that portrays people who have hurt others be allowed to remain? Should statues of those who bought and sold humans as slaves, for example, stand in the middle of cities? What about statues of those who simply bene-fitted from the trade? What about statues of those that knew about the trade but did nothing to stop it? How should we judge the morality of the subject of an art piece. Should art that depicts a person who cheated on their marriage, or a person who commanded soldiers into the death of war be allowed in our city?

When we start judging art by the morality of its subject we also need to think about the morality of its maker. If a beautiful piece of music is composed by a person who advocates violence and suffering, by someone who believes some humans deserve to be mistreated, should we still enjoy the music?

Can art be separated from its artist? Can art be separated from its subject? If I find beauty in something that is tragic, or violent, is that art? Some, for example, might argue that horror movies are beautiful. Or are we sabotaging Schiller's plan – and rather than shaping our soul by gazing on beauty, misshaping it by gazing on the ugly? Perhaps humans need to gaze at both to truly understand ourselves?

Can problematic and flawed humans create something that is sublime?

Conclusion

To fulfil your human nature, you decide to become an artist. You are inspired by pigeons. You decide to create a pink pigeon with spikes and chewing gum. You want this pigeon to represent the fearless nature of city pigeons. You work for months to build your 6-foot pigeon, including a hidden loudspeaker that makes pigeon noises – loud enough to scare any cat for miles.

Once finished you take this piece of art to the centre of your city for proud display. Some stand next to your art and think it is great. They take selfies. A couple try to get their dog on top of the pigeon. But a large group of people is dismayed. What is this? 'What is this monstrosity? I have never seen anything uglier' you hear a person say.

Another person looks at your pigeon and cries: 'This is an affront to the heavens'. 'This is not art', says a man with a severe moustache, 'it must be some vegan propaganda!' His statement confuses you. You never thought of veganism or food when making your art. Suddenly someone hurls a rock at your pigeon and screams it must be destroyed. People get quite upset about pigeons and you take your pigeon and go home.

What is art will never be a simple question. What is beautiful will never be agreed on. But we know that making art, and enjoying art, is a key part of being human. Therefore, our challenge is creating a world where we can create art – music, paintings, dance, gardening – and enjoy art, to express ourselves, to explore ideas, to get glimpses of the sublime.

Chapter Summary

In this chapter, we examined whether art can shape thinking by confronting people with the sublime, as philosophers such as Burke and Schiller have argued. As we explored how art can affect individuals, we questioned whether it is fair that only some people have the time and resources to make or enjoy art. We presented Rancière's argument that access to art is a matter of justice.

We also explored what constitutes art. We noted how those with power have historically been able to define what is beautiful and what is art. We discussed how technology might help make the creation and access to art more democratic. We noted that Hume argues that beauty is subjective while Bourdieu holds that society shapes ideas of beauty and art. We examined how controversial art challenges society's ideas of what is beautiful and normal. We raised the question of whether controversial art should be allowed to continue, or if there is a moral line – that neither the subject nor the creator of art – should cross?

Pondering Points

- Should the government spend money supporting art? If so, on what type of art and where do you think this art should be placed?
- Should art be censored to respect cultural values?
- Plato argued that art should be a mandatory part of education (although Plato censored what type and kind of art). Do you agree?
- During WWII museums went to great lengths to hide and safeguard art, to make sure it was not destroyed during bombing. Do you think this was correct, or would it have been better to spend those resources and thinking on saving lives?
- What piece of art (any type of art) has most impacted you. Why?

References

Argent, Lawrence. "I See What You Mean." In *Sculpture*. Denver, Colorado: Colorado Convention Center, 2005.

Aristotle. *"Metaphysics*. c. 350 BCE." Translated by W. D. Ross. In *The Complete Works of Aristotle: The Revised Oxford Translation*, edited by Jonathan Barnes. Princeton: Princeton University Press, 1984.

Berger, Martin A. *Sight Unseen: Whiteness and American Visual Culture*. Berkeley: University of California Press, 2005.

Boogaerdt, Hugo. " 'Helena' by Marco Evaristti." *Art Electronic Media*, March 24, 2010. www.web.archive.org/web/20110608000000*/http://www.artelectronicmedia.com/artwork/helena. (Accessed June 8, 2011).

Burke, Edmund. *A Philosophical Enquiry into the Origin of Our Ideas of the Sublime and Beautiful*. Project Gutenberg, 2008. www.gutenberg.org/ebooks/15043

Dewey, John. *Art as Experience*. New York: Perigee Books, 1980.

Duchamp, Marcel (anonymously). "The Richard Mutt Case." *The Blind Man*, no. 2 (May 1917).

Francioni, Francesco, and Federico Lenzerini. "The Destruction of the Buddhas of Bamiyan and International Law." *European Journal of International Law* 14, no. 4 (2003): 619–651.

Hume, David. *Of the Standard of Taste and Other Essays (1757)*. Edited by John W. Lenz. Indianapolis: Bobbs-Merrill, 1965.

Jobson, Christopher. "Artist Hubert Duprat Collaborates with Caddisfly Larvae as They Build Aquatic Cocoons from Gold and Pearls." *Colossal*, July 25, 2014. www.thisiscolossal.com/2014/07/hubert-duprat-caddisflies/.

Library of Congress. "Frederick Douglass and the Power of Pictures." *Picture This: Library of Congress Prints & Photos*, February 13, 2020. www.blogs.loc.gov/picturethis/2020/02/frederick-douglass-and-the-power-of-pictures/.

P55 Art. "The Influence of Marcel Duchamp's 'Fountain' on Art." *P55 Magazine*, November 19, 2021. www.p55.art/en/blogs/p55-magazine/the-influence-of-marcel-duchamps-fountain-on-art.

Plato. *Symposium*. 385–370 BCE. Translated by Alexander Nehamas and Paul Woodruff. Indianapolis: Hackett Publishing Company, 1989.

Plamper, Jan. *The Stalin Cult: A Study in the Alchemy of Power*. New Haven: Yale University Press, 2012.

Rancière, Jacques. *The Politics of Aesthetics: The Distribution of the Sensible*. Translated by Gabriel Rockhill. London: Continuum, 2004.

Ruskin, John. "The Nature of Gothic." In *The Stones of Venice, Volume II: The Sea-Stories*, 151–230. London: Smith, Elder & Co., 1853.

Schiller, Friedrich. *On the Aesthetic Education of Man* 1795. Translated by Elizabeth M. Wilkinson and L. A. Willoughby. Oxford: Clarendon Press, 1967.

Weiner, Eric. *The Geography of Genius: A Search for the World's Most Creative Places from Ancient Athens to Silicon Valley*. New York: Simon & Schuster, 2016.

Wikipedia contributors. "Meat dress of Lady Gaga." *Wikipedia*, The Free Encyclopedia. www.en.wikipedia.org/w/index.php?title=Meat_dress_of_Lady_Gaga&oldid=1231354738. (Accessed June 30, 2024).

18 Does the Past Affect the Future?

Questions About Colonialism, Knowledge, and Justice

Argentinian philosopher Enrique Dussel speaks up.

'If we want to improve our world, to seek justice and change, we need to decolonise our thinking. We cannot repeat what was done in the past, we cannot keep doing the same thing, in the same way, and expect something new, something different'.

Plato looks up from a chess game Marx and Sartre are playing. 'What does 'decolonise' mean?'

There is a short silence. So much meaning is contained in one small word. And so many debates about its meaning.

'Well', Dussel explains, 'colonisation, is when one state takes over another. However, colonisation has never been just about military control. It was, of course, also about political and economic control, *and* it was also about cultural control. To justify taking over another culture, the coloniser had to present their way of thinking, of being, as better, and those colonised as backward, ignorant, savage. So they took political, economic, and military control, but they also controlled how the culture they took over was presented. Or even if it was presented. Many times they simply tried to erase the culture that was there before'.

'Yes', Edward Said, a Palestinian philosopher continues, 'for example, look at how the Orient has been presented in history. Arabs…are thought of as camel-riding, terroristic, hook-nosed … whose undeserved wealth is an affront to real civilization'.[1]

Anibal Quijano, from Peru, jumps in, 'Most of us have grown up thinking that the ideas that grew from your writings,' he nods to Plato, 'from Western, Greco-Roman, and European thinkers, were the most civilised, the most advanced. The only way to think. Many still think this way, even after years of our countries being independent, this is what I call *coloniality* – we might be independent, but we still think as if we are controlled by the colonial power. We ignore ideas that were there before the colonial invasion and fail to see how pre-colonial ideas have stolen. We

DOI: 10.4324/9781032620121-23

see ourselves as less able, as less advanced. We see the world as the colonial powers wanted it to be seen, rather than as it really is'.

'Then, decoloniality', comes back in Plato, 'is working to see beyond the shadows of the colony, to consider again what is true, climbing out the cave that history might have put us in'.

Yes, I think, that is one way to think about Plato's Allegory of the Cave.[2] In seeking knowledge, we need to walk beyond the limits imposed on our knowledge by those who have historically held power. We need to rethink whose stories we have heard, and to wonder which stories we have not heard and question why.

Imagine being at home one evening, relaxing, maybe reading this book. Suddenly someone comes into your house. They come with guns. They explain that they are coming to save you, or to show you God, or to help your land develop. They demand to take control. They take the book you are reading and throw it away, saying it is filled with false information. They force you to leave your traditions, to forget your language, to start living in a different way. They burn your family albums, they change your name, they force you to forget who you are. You are forced to work for them. To speak like them. To dress like them. If you refuse you might be killed.

Many years later, you try to remember your language, try to remember the way you used to dress, what you used to do, before they came. You look up again at the stars and try to remember what they looked like before it all changed. You see the constellations they taught you but … you knew other constellations before. It is hard to remember. For so many years your language, your ideas, your traditions have been forbidden. You struggle to make the sounds of your language. You find that some of your ideas, your music, has been taken over by those who came. You find your friends mocking your attempts to remember, encouraging you to be modern and forget a useless past.

But you want to take it back. You want to remember your past, and you want justice for what was taken, what was destroyed. You realise there is great beauty and knowledge in these ancient ways of knowing, of being, and maybe even solutions for the problems of the present. But how can you get others to listen?

Decolonisation: A Short Definition

To understand decolonisation, we need to understand colonisation. Colonisation is the process of one state taking over another, controlling its population and imposing its rules. This is what happened during what is known as the 'Age of Exploration' or the 'Age of Discovery' – the period between the fifteenth and seventeenth centuries when European countries raced to expand their dominion over the rest of the world. But this was not the only era of colonisation. There was colonisation before that time and there has been colonisation after that time. Some, for example, argue that the USA has, and continues to, forced its culture, its language, its economic interests, and even its military in many parts of the world, particularly Latin America.

Decolonisation means working to revalue the ideas, languages, and cultures, that were repressed or devalued during colonisation. Because colonisation is a multifaceted process (it affects the political, the economic, the linguistic, the literary, the military ...) decolonisation is also a multifaceted project. It is about rethinking all aspects of our human reality with a critical lens[3] to understand how the history of colonisation has impacted us.

What Does Decolonisation Have to Do with Philosophy?

Decolonisation and philosophy intersect in two important ways: knowledge and justice.

Epistemology is the branch of philosophy that looks at knowledge. Philosophy asks us to consider what we know and how we know. Let's think back to Plato's Allegory of the Cave: this allegory can be read as the journey to find truth and knowledge. Most people are satisfied, according to Plato, with knowing only shadows, which are human creations, rather than the truth. Part of the process of colonisation is to impose one way of knowing and one set of beliefs, prohibiting any questioning – creating a set of shadows that all people have to submit to. Colonisation meant ignoring, forbidding, or destroying the knowledge of the colonised – and with it the possibility of questioning what was known or how it was known.

Philosophy further asks us to consider *how* we learn things, whose knowledge we value and why. Māori Philosopher Linda Tuhiwai Smith notes that western scientific knowledge has not only ignored other knowledges, but it has also been developed by abusing indigenous people. Non-white bodies have been used – dead and alive – for research, without permission and without concern for pain or trauma. To advance scientific knowledge, for example, experiments have been conducted on the bodies of indigenous people, and people of colour, without concern for their suffering.[4]

Research has historically been abusive. Imagine if someone came into your house, asked all sorts of questions about your family, your ancestors, took pictures of you, measured you and your family – all without asking you for permission ... and then left to never be seen again. This has been the case of much of research. Researchers from the 'Global North'[5] descend on the villages of people in the 'Global South' who kindly receive them. They ask questions, they measure things, they take samples, and then they leave. Academics get paid and receive prestige for their research. The people they research get nothing.

They are not even asked if they want to participate, or how they would want to participate.[6]

Meanwhile, the knowledge of indigenous people has been dismissed as useless or unscientific. Kenyan thinker Ngũgĩ wa Thiong'o has noted how indigenous languages have been ignored and suffocated in educational systems that are run in the language of the conquerors. Failing to use the native language means failing to acknowledge a non-western way of thinking about reality. Indigenous people's knowledge of the local environment, of their bodies, of truth and justice, has been ignored. It is only recently, as we face a climate crisis, that western institutions have begun to listen to indigenous people's knowledge about the environment in our desperate search to withstand the crisis and avoid human annihilation.

Finally, philosophy and decolonisation also overlap in the realm of ethics. *Ethics* is the philosophical study of what is morally right, what is just. Philosophy, therefore, challenges us to consider if colonisation was/is just and what is the just way to act now, in response to colonial acts. There are many aspects to this question. For example, considering distributive justice, we might ask should the descendants of colonisers pay back for what their ancestors took? Can justice work through time? Or do colonising countries owe aid and support to the countries they benefited from?[7] But, as we have mentioned, colonisation is not just about economics and politics. It is also about ideas – what ideas were presented, what ideas were erased – and humans: how humans were treated. Thus, we might ask what is a just way to discuss what colonisation was? Is it just to judge colonial powers by our current moral norms? Should those in the present feel responsible for what their ancestors did in the past? Should we acknowledge benefits that came from the colonial process, while also acknowledging the abuse, thieving, and murders that were part of the process?

The Psychological and Ethical Impact of Decolonisation

One of the most controversial aspects of decolonisation is the idea that decolonisation needs to happen *inside* a person, in our mind. Psychiatrist Frantz Fanon argued that the most nefarious or dangerous aspect of colonisation is the impact it has on the psychology of the person. Colonisation is based on the idea that those who colonise are better, in some way, to those who are colonised. This is the logic that justifies colonisation. The colonisers are presented as more advanced, or civilised, or wiser, or braver, or closer to God. Logically, then, the colonised are presented as the opposite: backward, dumber, cowardly, heathens.

Now, consider the impact of growing up within this set up. If you are the colonised, you grow up in a system that tells you daily you are less – less smart, less brave, less beautiful … and if you are part of the colonised group, you grow up every day feeling the power and prestige of being part of the 'better' group.

Feeling less would hurt your self-esteem. You might become angry and depressed. Or you might look for ways to improve yourself. Since the colonisers are presented as 'better', you might try to be more like them to improve yourself. You will try to speak like them, to dress like them, to think like them. Fanon noted how when colonialism lined up with skin colour – the colonisers light skinned, the colonised dark skinned – then those with dark skin might come to hate their skin, to want to be white. This is the basis of his book *Black Skins White Masks.*

The idea of hating your own skin, of wanting to be, to look like someone else, is atrocious. The psychological impact of colonialism is, therefore, of serious concern. French Tunisian Albert Memmi noted that colonisation dehumanised both the coloniser and the colonised. To justify their actions the colonisers must constantly deny the humanity of those they oppressed, they have to act in ways that are morally unjust. Thus, they are morally and psychologically destroyed. They are dishonest with themselves and live in fear of having their lies discovered, of having their superiority questioned. The colonised, on the other hand, grow up hating themselves and resenting what they cannot have. It is a dangerous and unhealthy psychological recipe.

When an empire ends, people don't suddenly wake up and stop thinking of each other as better/worse. Those who have been told they were lesser and therefore needed to be controlled, guided, helped, and colonised, might still see themselves as less. They might still try to be like those who conquered them. Or they might seek revenge for all they suffered. Those who were in control, might still look down on others, see them as less. This is what Anibal Quijano refers to as *coloniality* – the empires might have ended, but their psychological impact continues.

How can these ideas be changed? How can those who think and feel less, make themselves feel better? How can those who have grown up in power come to terms with the idea that they are no better than those they used to control? Even more, how can those who abused others come to terms with the cruelty and wrongness of their actions? This is perhaps the biggest challenge of decolonisation.

Guilt and Fragility

One of the reasons decolonisation has been opposed is that it makes people feel uncomfortable. Being told that your success in life is in part the result of unfair systems that gave people who look like you an advantage, while hurting others, is uncomfortable. We might ask whether this is fair – is it fair to blame people for what their ancestors might have done? In the USA there have been challenges to educational material that brings up history in a way that might make students feel uncomfortable. But we might ask with Plato, isn't leaving the cave always an uncomfortable experience?

Decolonisation campaigners have also asked for statues of those who supported and/or benefited from colonial systems to be brought down. They have asked for traditions that were based on mocking or dehumanising others – such as blackface – to be ended. In response some have argued that these actions fail to appreciate the good those people brought to the world, or how these traditions are part of cultures that also have beauty. There is disagreement on how to present history: should colonisers, for example, be seen as courageous explorers, or as violent thieves? Can we understand history in a more complicated way and see these people as both – adventurous, brave, and avaricious and brutal?

Many questions of justice emerge: what is a just way to understand and represent the past? Are the feelings of those hurt by the past more important than the feelings of those being hurt in the present? How can justice for the past avoid injustices in the present? Perhaps Edward Said's words need to be heeded here:

> *You cannot continue to victimize someone else just because you yourself were a victim once—there has to be a limit.*

Museums

Walking into the British Museum is an awe-inspiring experience. Suddenly out of the chaos of London, you are in a large, airy space that holds treasures from all over the world, from across history. The Rosetta Stone is here – an ancient Egyptian stone with parallel inscriptions that allowed the translation of hieroglyphic text. The Parthenon Sculptures are also here – Greek sculptures that once decorated ancient Athens. Mexican codices, holding information about Aztec culture and history. And Hao Hakananai's statue from East Island (Rapa Nui). Until recently, Benin bronze art was also hosted here.

But why are these treasures here? Have people around the world agreed to donate or lend their treasures to this place? No, in fact there have been many requests to have these items returned to their place of origin. Some of these treasures are sacred to their creators. The Hao Hakananai is sacred to the people of Rapa Nui, holding the spirit of their ancestor, and its return is demanded. Benin Bronzes are being repatriated to Nigeria; these were looted from the Kingdom of Benin by British forces.

In 2023 the British Museum was in the news when several objects in its collection were discovered missing or stolen. The irony of this was not lost on many who asked – aren't most of the objects the British Museum holds in fact stolen? How is stealing *from* the museum different from stealing *for* the museum?

Museum debates demonstrate the challenges of decolonisation. Many of the objects they hold were stolen by colonising armies because they could – might makes right – without regard for their owners. Should the museum now return these objects? These objects are the material legacies of colonised cultures – they are their history and their knowledge. They belong to the heirs of these cultures. Is it ever just to steal and keep what belongs to others?

The safety of the objects is often cited as an argument against repatriation of these objects: in the museum, the argument goes, the objects are safe. This argument, however, is based on ideas that supported colonialism: non-Europeans are less developed, less safe, more violent, less able to appreciate or guard art and science. The argument is illogical given that these objects were made by the very cultures seen as lacking the knowledge to keep them safe – and were stolen by the West.

The danger to historical artifacts due to violence, however, is worth considering[8] – but it might happen in any part of the world! Is this an argument about safety or about ownership? Philosopher Kwame Anthony Appiah has argued that art should be considered a human, rather than a national treasure. It should be held in a place safe for all humans to see and treasure. Moreover, as no culture is isolated, and cultures are porous and learn from each other, it would be impossible to say that an object belongs to one single culture. To whom, then, should these objects be returned – to the governments of the countries that are now in charge of the areas where these cultures once flourished? To local communities? To contemporary artists?

Conclusion and This Book

Decolonisation requires thinking critically about where our information comes from, why we think in a certain way, who we listen to, who we ignore, and why we behave as we do. As you might have noted, this book explores many ideas presented and developed by philosophers who participated and benefited from colonial exploits. The book has sought to bring in other voices into its conversation – philosophers from the Global South, female philosophers – but is this enough? Have we done enough to acknowledge the terrible deeds – whether by action or omission – of the philosophers in the past? Have we understood their limitations?

Knowledge is a human treasure, it is a human project; knowledge builds by learning from others, by being challenged. But we must acknowledge that we have gotten to this point in our knowledge journey in part by stealing knowledge, by hurting others to gain knowledge, and that we have also ignored much knowledge. Perhaps this is where we need to start seeking wisdom, not just knowledge: by acknowledging past injustices and learning humbly from others.[9]

Chapter Summary

This chapter has discussed colonisation and decolonisation. Philosophers of decolonisation, such as Enrique Dussel, Anibal Quijano, and Ngũgĩ wa Thiong'o, note that colonial empires impacted not just economic and political structures in the countries they took over, but also how people thought about themselves, thought about who should lead, and thought about what knowledge is valid. Ngũgĩ Wa Thiong'o notes that even language is affected by colonisation, with local languages forbidden or seen as inferior and unworthy of being taught. Fanon and Memmi focus on the psychological impact of colonisation, which leads the colonised to see themselves as lesser, or to resent who they are, while it makes colonisers into monsters who abuse fellow humans on the basis of lies. We have discussed museums as an example of institutions that are challenged by decolonisation as we consider the just way to handle artifacts that were stolen by colonial powers in the past. The chapter notes that decolonisation is central to philosophy as it focuses our attention on knowledge and justice, two key aspects of political philosophy.

Pondering Points

- Do you think museum should return artifacts to their place of origin? Why or why not?
- How has colonisation affected you?
- How can we address injustices of the past without committing injustices in the present?

References

Bogdanos, Matthew. "The Casualties of War: The Truth about the Iraq Museum." *American Journal of Archaeology* 109, no. 3 (2005): 477–526.

Cockburn, Patrick. "Isis Executes Respected Archaeologist in Palmyra and Hangs His Body from Ancient Ruins He Devoted His Life to Restoring." *The Independent*, August 19, 2015. www.independent.co.uk/news/world/middle-east/isis-executes-archaeologist-in-palmyra-before-hanging-his-body-from-ancient-ruins-he-devoted-his-life-to-restoring-10461601.html.

Cunliffe, Emma. "Archaeological Site Damage in the Cycle of War and Peace: A Syrian Case Study." *Journal of Eastern Mediterranean Archaeology & Heritage Studies* 3, no. 2 (2015): 229–247.

Dussel, Enrique. *Philosophy of Liberation.* Translated by Aquilina Martinez and Christine Morkovsky. Maryknoll, NY: Orbis Books, 1985.

Fanon, Frantz. *Black Skin, White Masks.* Translated by Charles Lam Markmann. London: Pluto Press, 1986.

Fanon, Frantz. *The Wretched of the Earth.* Translated by Constance Farrington. New York: Grove Press, 1963.

Gregory, James. "British Museum Facing Social Media Campaign to Return Easter Island Statue." *BBC News*, February 18, 2024. www.bbc.co.uk/news/world-latin-amer ica-68332824.

Memmi, Albert. *The Colonizer and the Colonized.* Translated by Howard Greenfeld. Boston: Beacon Press, 1967.

Moore, Jason W. "'This Lofty Mountain of Silver Could Conquer the Whole World': Potosí and the Political Ecology of Underdevelopment, 1545–1800." *The Journal of Philosophical Economics* 4, no. 1 (2010): 58–103.

Nuriddin, A., G. Mooney, and A. I. R. White. "Reckoning with Histories of Medical Racism and Violence in the USA." *Lancet* 396, no. 10256 (2020): 949–951. https://doi.org/10.1016/S0140-6736(20)32032-8.

Quijano, Aníbal. "Coloniality of Power, Eurocentrism, and Latin America." *Nepantla: Views from South* 1, no. 3 (2000): 533–580.

Said, Edward W. *Orientalism.* New York: Pantheon Books, 1978.

Smith, Linda Tuhiwai. *Decolonizing Methodologies: Research and Indigenous Peoples.* 2nd ed. London: Zed Books, 2012.

Thiong'o, Ngũgĩ wa. *Decolonising the Mind: The Politics of Language in African Literature.* London: James Currey, 1986.

Titi, Catharine. "The British Museum and the Marbles." In *The Parthenon Marbles and International Law.* Cham: Springer, 2023. https://doi.org/10.1007/978-3-031-26357-6_6.

Tythacott, Louise, and Kostas Arvanitis, eds. *Museums and Restitution: New Practices, New Approaches.* London: Routledge, 2016.

19 How Can We Build a Just World?

Questions About Justice, Diversity, and the Future

You decide to take a break from the intense conversations in our philosophers' party and go for a walk. You are deep in your contemplation of whether we could make the world better by redistributing resources or by getting rid of governments when you hear some strange noises. Intrigued, you follow the sounds and find a little child who has fallen into a dirty pond. The child is struggling to get out, weighted down by some trash. If someone does not help soon, the child will drown. You are wearing a brand-new outfit and holding an expensive new phone. Will you step into the dirty pond and save the child?

The example of a drowning child is a thought experiment by philosopher Peter Singer to help us think about our responsibility to help others. Most people, we can assume, would agree that helping the child, even if it ruins your outfit, is the right thing to do. The value of a child's life is hardly comparable to the worth of clothes or other material things.

Now, imagine the child was in a pond further away. You might not be able to get to the drowning child, but you could send someone to help the child. You could make a call and send money – the equivalent of the cost of your outfit – to pay for the car needed to go and save the child. Would you do this? Again, most of us would probably say yes. If you know a child is drowning, you don't just scroll on your phone instead of sending the money needed to save them.

Singer asks us to think about a child who is not drowning, but starving, or homeless. Does this change the right thing to do? Should we not still help?

When we think about building a better, more just world, we must consider what we are responsible for. Are we responsible for helping people around the world, or only our fellow citizens? And what does helping mean?

DOI: 10.4324/9781032620121-24

Cake or Distributive Justice

Imagine you have a cake. You did not make it. It appeared before you as if by magic – poof! A delicious strawberry cake! Perfect timing as well, as you are so hungry! What a great treat to have. But, um, could you share a bit with me please? And also, perhaps, a bit with my dog Flash? He particularly likes cake (as you can tell by the way he is sitting in a small pool of drool over here). Could you also give a bit to our friend Erwin who has just arrived?

What would be a just or fair way to distribute the cake?

I suggest you split the cake into 4ths – one fourth for each of us. Equality. 'What!' Erwin cries upsets, 'You are not going to give the same amount to a dog as to us!'. My dog takes great offence at this and howls. Why should a dog have less than a human, he seems to be asking. He lays down under the table, looking sad.

On the other hand, you note that Erwin had a massive lunch just before joining us, while you have not had food since yesterday because you have been so busy reading and thinking about philosophy. If you don't have some food soon, you might faint or be unwell. Surely you should get a bigger piece because you need it more, and Erwin should be happier with a smaller piece since he is not hungry. 'What?', Erwin complains again, 'what I ate before has nothing to do with this cake. It is not my fault you have not eaten.' That reminds me, I am writing this book, which takes lots of work, so maybe you should give me more cake?

What is a fair way to distribute the cake: everyone gets the same, the hungriest person gets more, the hardest working person gets more, humans get more than dogs ... or is there some other, more just way to share the cake?

The Veil of Ignorance

What we are discussing here is distributive justice. The cake, of course, is just an example of resources that humans share – like wealth or oil. Philosopher John Rawls proposed a thought experiment to help us think about the just way to distribute resources and treat others fairly.

Imagine that I show you a very light, shimmery, cloth. This veil, I explain, is magical. You don't believe me but when I put the veil over you, you immediately forget who you are. You do *not* forget anything about the world we live in, but you don't know who you are. This is how the *veil of ignorance* works. When you step behind it (or when I put it over you!) you forget who you are. You don't know if you are a child, or a 92-year-old person. You don't know what your gender is. You don't know if you are homeless, or a billionaire. You do not know if you live in a cabin by the woods in the USA, in a sky scrapper in Kuala Lumpur, or in a favela in Brazil. You do, however, remember what you know about our world. You know there is poverty in our world, inequality, injustices. You know we do not live in a utopia.

This place, where you know about the world, but do not know who you are, is what Rawls called the *original position*. Rawls argued that it is from this position that we can best seek justice – because we are not biased when we make our decisions. We cannot decide what is best for us or our family, because we do not know who we are.

Let's go back to the cake example. Behind the veil of ignorance, in the original position, you do not know if you are you, me, or Erwin. You do not know if you are rich and have cakes made for you every day, or if you are a starving child who has never had the luxury of tasting a sweet. All you know is that there is a cake that needs to be shared and you want to share the cake in such a way that when you come out from behind the veil you would be happy with the outcome – whether you have billions, are Erwin, or are struggling with poverty.

Now if we are talking about wealth, rather than cake, what would be the fair way to distribute wealth? If you are a billionaire, you might not be happy if taxes took all your money – but you might be ok if a small percentage is taken, and you are left with most. Or not. If you are poor, you might think that it is unfair that people with more billions than they need refuse to share a portion of that to help you buy food. This is why, Rawls argues, we can only make a fair decision if we do not know who we are. Linking back to our first example, you don't know if you are the child in the pond, or the person who can step in and save the child.

In our cake discussion, my dog Flash joined in to ask for some cake. Rawls' thought experiment does not include animals, but we could expand his thinking to include them. If you were not a human, would you be happy with how humans have shared resources around the world? Would it be more just to consider other living beings, from pets to whales and snails, when deciding how we use our planet?

Rawls' Principles

Let's go back to the cake. From behind the veil, how would you choose to distribute the cake? Flash, as a dog shouldn't really have cake. Much as he likes it, it is not good for him. People who need food to survive need to take priority. Those who are already fed could still get some cake, but theirs is a want, not a need, so their priority is lower. So you *might* decide to distribute the cake in a way that is not equal, but that is fair.

Rawls argued that if we think about multiple examples like this, we will come to see that justice is not always equality. Sometimes justice is difference. For example, if someone is starving, it is fair to give that person more. If a country is suffering from drought, it is just to send water to them and to not send water to a country that has access to fresh water.

Rawls, therefore, argues that equality is not always justice. Some might need more; some might need something different. To be just we cannot treat everyone the same.

Utilitarianism and Consequentialism

You are thinking about examples when treating people justly does not mean treating them equally, as argued by Rawls, when you start thinking about your family. At night your family chooses a movie to watch, but you must always watch something that is appropriate for the youngest. When you go out, you must always consider the youngest's naptimes. This is unequal, but your family argues that it is fair. You argue back: what about choosing activities or movies that the *majority* would be happy with? Even if the youngest is unhappy? Surely the happiness of the majority is more important than the need of a minority? You are presenting a utilitarian view.

Utilitarian philosophers, such as Jeremy Bentham, argue that justice should seek to provide the greatest happiness for the greatest number. For Bentham, figuring out the right way to act was a bit like maths; you need to add the happiness an action brings and subtract the sadness it causes. But if dropping a bomb on a city of 10,000 ends a war that would kill one million, thus creating happiness for at least a million, versus sadness for 10,000, would this be just? Bentham might disagree with the calculation of happiness, I am presenting or *felicific calculus*, as he called it. We might debate whether deaths cause greater unhappiness than lives saved. The maths gets complicated. Some actions bring pure happiness – seeing someone you love laugh – but some actions bring happiness and unhappiness (finishing a good book, or doing hard work), or happiness at first and then sadness later – such as, perhaps, attacking a military target.

Niccolo Machiavelli, a sixteenth-century philosopher, might argue that bombing a city, despite its terrible cost, would be just if its consequences are good. Machiavelli followed what is known as *consequentialist ethics*. He argued that the 'ends justify the means'. This was one of the arguments used to justify the use of atomic bombs in Japan during WWII. This logic is still used by some governments to justify hurting civilians to combat terrorism.

But do the ends justify doing *anything*? For example, we might agree that there is a global environmental crisis. One of the ways in which we could address this crisis is to cut humanity in half. Would solving the climate crises justify killing half of humanity?[1] Perhaps, less drastically, governments could simply force people to live only from what they can grow in their garden, ending all mass consumption, and maybe only allow some people to have children. Again, would sustainability justify such authoritarian policies, limiting people's freedom and choices?[2]

Deontological Versus Virtue Ethics

Some philosophers argue that actions are just or unjust regardless of their consequences. Dropping a bomb on civilians, for example, is unjust. They are not combatants. Whether this stops or expands warfare is a secondary consideration. It is unjust for a military to kill civilians. Period. Similarly, it is unjust for governments to kill their population, regardless of the justification they might give.

Immanuel Kant is known for his support of deontological ethics – that is ethics that hold that there are right and wrong actions, regardless of their consequences. Kant argued we should behave in a way that allows our choices to become universal rules. For example, if killing is bad, then it is always bad. If lying is bad, it is always bad. Kant argued that humans should never be treated as objects to be used toward a goal. Each person is a subject and must be treated as such. In our example above, killing humans to obtain sustainability or to end a war is wrong because humans should not be treated as tools to achieve an end goal – they are ends in themselves.

Elisabeth Anscombe disagreed with Kant. For Anscombe how we decide to act cannot be based on simple rules. Rather ethics should be guided by our moral character. For example, Kant might argue that killing is always wrong, but what if you see a terrorist about to kill a group of innocent people. Is it not just at this point to be brave and stop or, if necessary, kill the terrorist to save the lives of the innocent? Is your intention to save the innocent not worth considering when we think about whether your actions were just?[3]

Do We Sacrifice Ourselves for Others?

Imagine you are on a boat with your friends and see someone drowning. Surely you should pull the drowning person up and save them. But wait, there are two people. Ok, pull out both. But what if there were many more people drowning? If you pull more people out, your boat might sink. Should you save those drowning or save your own boat? If you can only save a few of those drowning, how would you choose?

One of the greatest challenges when considering how to act justly is deciding what to do when an action might hurt you or others. It is easy, and correct, to save a child if the cost of this is ruining your outfit – however much you might have loved your unicorn-hair shoes. But it is a different question when saving a child might cost you your life, or might put the life of your own child in harm's way. What is a just action then?

Justice a Quick Review and Application to Breaking the Social Contract

So far this chapter has looked at different frameworks, or ideas, of what just behaviour is. Each of these frameworks offers a guide on how to behave justly:

- Rawls argues that we should choose from behind the veil of ignorance, aiming for fairness, not equality.

- Utilitarian philosophers like Bentham argue that we should seek the greatest good for the greatest number.
- Consequentialist philosophers like Machiavelli argue that we should base our actions on their consequences: the ends justify whatever we need to do to get there.
- Deontological philosophers like Kant argue that our actions should be guided by unchanging universal rules.
- Virtue ethicists like Elizabeth Anscombe argue that our behaviour should be guided by moral virtues such as courage, empathy, and generosity.

Using these frameworks can help us understand the challenges of choosing a just action in different scenarios. Using these frameworks, for example, you could think about whether we should limit peoples' freedom to solve climate change, or whether we should redistribute wealth to help the poor.

What about those who break the rules a society agrees on? For example, if we agree that killing is wrong, would this mean that the death penalty is always wrong by deontological principles? Or should punishment be based on its consequences, regardless of its means? If we kill a criminal, they can no longer commit crimes. Or would it be just to torture a prisoner if this meant gaining information that can prevent further crimes?

One of the oldest legal systems we have record of, the Code of Hammurabi from Ancient Mesopotamia, presented justice as an 'eye for an eye' – that is, if someone hurt you, hurting them back would be justice. In a literal interpretation of this quote, however, we might ask how having two people partially blinded makes society better.

What we are discussing is retribution. If someone has broken our social contract, should justice focus on revenge, making those hurt feel better; on deterrence, stopping future crime; or on reformation, changing the person who broke the law to see the error of their ways? What is the most just way?

Jeremy Bentham proposed a prison system which, he argued, would work best for society. He called this the *Panopticon*. The Panopticon had a tall guard tower and all the prisoners' cells around this tower. The tower would be designed in such a way that, while the guards could look out and see into the cells of the prisoners, the prisoners could not see into the tower. This meant that the prisoners could never know when the guards were there, or when the guards were looking at them. Since the prisoners don't know when the guards are looking at them, they assume the guards might look at them at any moment. They start to guard themselves, imagining the guards looking at them all the time.

While Bentham's panopticon focused on a physical prison, we could consider whether our society teaches us to guard ourselves about certain behaviours. We internalise judgement. For example, we learn that people might judge us if we don't help an elderly person cross the street ... but they do not judge us if we order more food than we can eat and throw it out. What ideas about what is just have you internalised from your society?

Diversity and Justice

Different societies have different understandings of what justice is. A religious community, for example, might see its religious doctrine as providing a guide for justice, leading to a deontological perspective.[4] If two societies have different views on the right way to proceed on an issue, seeking a compromise will be challenging.

Indigenous justice refers to the justice system indigenous people had before colonisation. In some countries, as part of decolonisation,[5] indigenous communities have been given back the right to legislate on justice in their territory. In other words, they can decide what rules are in place, and how people who break these rules should be treated. They can decide what is a just way to act in their territory. But, as with religious groups, this creates a challenge: if two systems of justice disagree – such as the national system, and the indigenous system, or the national system and a religious system – which should take precedence? Which rules should rule?

Indigenous philosophers like Franke Wilmer (Cherokee), and Patricia Monture-Angus (Mohawk), argue that we need to rethink justice. For justice to be just, for us to create a just world, we need to listen to all voices. Perhaps we should not think of the state as the ultimate authority of what is just. Perhaps communities, such as indigenous nations, should choose their own justice which might go beyond considering property or ownership, to consider justice for nature and justice toward ancestors and dependants. Perhaps we should consider ideas of global justice.

Conclusion

Creating a better world means creating a more just world. However, the idea of justice is anything but simple. What rules are just, how to apply these rules justly, and how to deal with those who break the rules, are questions that political philosophers of every age and culture have discussed. There is one rule we find in one way or the other in multiple cultures and times: treat others as you would like to be treated. Perhaps if we could be kind to ourselves, and extend that kindness to others our world would head toward justice.

Chapter Summary

This chapter has explored the idea of justice. It has considered distributive justice within the state and at an international level, looking at the ideas of Peter Singer and John Rawls. We have discussed different frameworks for justice: Bentham and utilitarianism, Machiavelli and consequentialism, Kant and deontological ethics, and Anscombe and virtue ethics. The chapter has used these various ethical frameworks to consider different ethical challenges such as war and climate change. The chapter also considered just ways to address rule breaking, considering Hammurabi's code and Bentham's Panopticon. Ultimately the chapter noted that there is no universal understanding on justice. Indigenous philosophers such as Franke Wilmer and Patricia Monture-Angus have argued that indigenous peoples' ideas of justice need to be considered and we need to consider moving away from the state as the only definer of justice. In our search for justice, we must explore all frameworks of justice critically and thoughtfully.

Pondering Points

- Do you do what is right because it is right or because you are worried about getting in trouble? Plato explored this question by telling the story of the ring of Gyges. This is a ring that makes it wearer invisible. If you were invisible, would you do anything you would not do otherwise?
- If you could alter people through surgery in such a way that when they woke up they would never act unkindly again, would you do it? Why or why not?
- Is there anything you think should never, ever be done? What about something that should always be done, no matter what?

References

Anscombe, G. E. M. "Modern Moral Philosophy." *Philosophy* 33, no. 124 (1958): 1–19.

Bentham, Jeremy. *An Introduction to the Principles of Morals and Legislation.* Oxford: Clarendon Press, 1907. First published 1789.

Bentham, Jeremy. "Panopticon; Or The Inspection-House." In *The Works of Jeremy Bentham*, edited by John Bowring. Project Gutenberg, Vol. 4. 2011. www.gutenb erg.org/files/40129/40129-h/40129-h.htm#PANOPTICON_OR_THE_INSPECT ION-HOUSE.

Hammurabi. *The Code of Hammurabi.* Translated by L. W. King. The Avalon Project: Code of Hammurabi (yale.edu). [Online] https://avalon.law.yale.edu/ancient/ hamframe.asp (Accessed September 2024).

Kant, Immanuel. *Groundwork of the Metaphysics of Morals.* Translated and edited by Mary Gregor. Cambridge, MA: Cambridge University Press, 1998.

Lappi-Seppälä, Tapio. "Penal Policy in Scandinavia." *Crime and Justice* 36, no. 1 (2007): 217–295.

Machiavelli, Niccolò. *The Prince*. Translated by Harvey C. Mansfield. 2nd ed. Chicago: University of Chicago Press, 1998. First published 1532.

Monture-Angus, Patricia. *Thunder in My Soul: A Mohawk Woman Speaks*. Halifax: Fernwood Publishing, 1995.

Rawls, John. *A Theory of Justice*. Revised ed. Cambridge, MA: Harvard University Press, 1999.

Singer, Peter. "Famine, Affluence, and Morality." *Philosophy & Public Affairs* 1, no. 3 (1972): 229–243.

Wilmer, Franke. *The Indigenous Voice in World Politics: Since Time Immemorial*. Newbury Park: Sage Publications, 1993.

Until We Meet Again

20 Conclusion

The night is coming to an end. Everybody has had as much cake as humanly (or Yoda) possible. Socrates has danced for hours. There have been a great number of fascinating conversations. But the spacetime vortex we created to bring philosophers together is fading. Soon philosophers will return to their own space and time. This discussion will be forgotten except for what is in this book. What conclusions can we reach from it all?

Clearly, there is no easy path to a utopia. Our world is complicated. Our reality is made by the words we speak, by the art we create, by the governments we establish, by the value we give property, by how we decide to punish rule breakers, by how we relate to nature … to make our world a better place there are so many areas we need to consider. We need to think about what we want our future to be like and to decide how to resolve injustices from the past.

Perhaps this is the trickiest part: in our search for a better world, we are not starting from scratch. And we do not have magic. If we were starting from scratch, we could design the world exactly as needed – distribute people around the world, put a cap on fossil fuel use from the beginning, put art on every wall … or whatever else you think is right. But we are starting from where we are. It is hard. People are already on the planet. We already have poverty and pollution. We have had injustices. If we had a magic wand we could simply – poof! Make the problems disappear, or make people forget the past, or make extinct animals reappear …

Perhaps we can take a few last lessons from philosophers as we decide how to move forward.

Ideologies Are Dangerous

Ideologies are sets of ideas or beliefs that claim to explain the past and give guidance for the present, promising a certain future. Hannah Arendt states that 'Ideologies are harmless, uncritical and arbitrary opinions only as long as they are not believed in seriously'.

DOI: 10.4324/9781032620121-26

When we believe any idea to be completely correct, unquestionable, we head to dangerous ground. This is where we stop thinking critically, questioning, and instead start defending our ideas, even using violence.

There is no simple path to a better world. Seeking perfection is silly or, even worse, dangerous.

Since we cannot seek perfection, perhaps we should look to Aristotle and seek a golden mean. That is, seek a path of balance in our attempts. To not be so generous that we are left with nothing and not to be so stingy that we watch others starve while we sit on ur treasure. Or to seek balance between a country seeking peace, and a country preparing for war.

If we review what the book has discussed we will note that political theory is all about this balance, this grey zone between two extremes. Should we look for the interests of individuals, or the interest of the community? The interests of the present of those of the future? The interests of the state or the interests of groups within a state such as communities or nationalities.

Be critical of all ideas

This book has brought the ideas, and wisdom, and the mistakes of philosophers across time and around the world to consider the challenges we face and to think about the future we want to build. One of the key lessons we must learn is to be critical of all these ideas – consider their source, their reasoning, their impact. And to listen to the voices that have been ignored or silenced. Philosophical wisdom is not limited to ancient Greece, to Europe, or to the past. To solve complex problems, we need to consider all wisdom.

Technology, nature, and humanity

Our challenges are more urgent than those of people who came before us. Humans throughout history have considered to what extent they should explore science and use technology – at what point will machines take over? At what point will science destroy us? We can find this discussion in Frankenstein – will science be able to make new humans, and will these humans be monsters? – and centuries before when, for example, the Greeks discussed whether Prometheus should have given humans the power of technology (fire). But now we face AI. AI is developing at such fast speed, it is difficult to imagine where we will be 10, 50 years from now. And, again, we confront the questions: will machines take us over? Are we creating new monsters?

Hope and human nature

Humans have also considered the relation between us and the rest of nature since we started writing ... but our relationship with nature is now in crisis. If we do not change our behaviour, we are facing the end of humanity.

How do we address the crises we face? There are, of course, many others. Crises of justice as the inequalities of the past return to haunt us. Crises of violence by states and non-state actors, which sow seeds for future discord. What we face is not simple.

However, the wonder of humans, a wise person once told me, is hope. We don't just keep going blindly. Even though we rationally and emotionally understand the incredible challenge ahead, we still believe. We try against all odds. It is our hope that has led us to explore every part of this world seeking to find more beauty, more wonder, more possibilities. It is our hope that leads us to seek peace and trust forgiveness – to give others one more chance. It is our hope that makes us believe we can. It is our hope that leads us to fill pages like this with text, hoping that someone else will read these words and be inspired to keep going. Hope is what makes us human.

And I have great hope in young people. I know they are fearless. Brilliant. Hard working. I know they will look at these challenges and get to work. Be creative, be brave, be courageous. Learn from the past but understand that the past was also deeply mistaken and you must do better. We must do better. We will do better.

Si se puede, civil rights activists Cesar Chavez once said. And I believe it. *Yes, we can.*

After the party I find little scribbles on napkins from various philosophers.[1]
I transcribe these for you here:

Upset I didn't get a word in the book - not sure what the zeitgeist (spirit of the time) of this strange time is - questioning the past and seeking creative solutions? Hegel

Had a great time dancing — must remember to ask Zizek how they get bubbles in the water. Socrates

If leaders joined conversations like our party - and took these seriously - the planet would be in a better place. Philosophers for rulers, I say. Plato

There can be no utopia without respect of individual rights — Nozick

The real, and difficult, utopia, is deciding what life you want to live - Sartre

I am annoyed I was not allowed to eat my cake in peace - Hobbes
I like this phrase my friend James Madison shared with me 'If men were angels, no government would be necessary. If angels were to govern men, neither external nor internal controls on government would be necessary.' (Hobbes, again)

To change the world, we need to change education — let people think, don't make them memorise! Freire

To think wisely about how to make just laws - stand behind the veil of ignorance. Rawls

Access to art is about justice. A better world would give us all access to art! Ranciere

There is one humanity - separating into countries makes us forget this - Marcus Aurelius

Utopia, or sumak kawsay, living well, will only come when we see humans as part of nature — Acosta

Don't let others tell you, you are less. Utopia cannot be built that way- Fanon

Listen to the voices that are quiet, that speak differently, that do not sound 'philosophical' (Spivak).

These philosophers and me, not so different: we want walks, food, safe, adventures, and cuddles. That is goods life -signed, Flash, The Dog.

Notes

Time Traveling to Party with Philosophers

1 Tahuatinsuyo or Tawantinsuyo was the name of the great Inca empire. Tahuatinsuyo means 'four regions'.

2 I am referring here to Kopi Luwak or civet coffee. This is coffee made from coffee beans which have been eaten and pooped by the Asian palm civet – an Asian mammal that looks like a koala and cat combined.

3 Esperanto is a language created by Dr L.L. Zamenhof, using English, French, German, Greek, Italian, Latin, Polish, Russian, and Yiddish as a basis, with a grammar that has been compared to Chinese. The idea of Esperanto was to create a language that everyone could speak – a universal language, not owned by anyone – to create harmony across the world. To do this Esperanto avoids irregular verbs, and gendered words, and its writing is entirely phonetic. No secret silent letters!

4 Unless noted otherwise, these conversations are entirely fictional, based on my understanding of philosophers' ideas, actions, and personalities, whether dead or alive.

5 The Socratic method is a method of learning by asking questions. This is what Socrates did: he asked more and more questions to help people consider their assumptions and find errors in their logic. Needless to say, some people found this rather annoying. They did not like constantly being questioned. And realising that what you thought was right is based on false premises or prejudices is rather embarrassing … Constantly asking questions got Socrates into trouble and eventually led to him being given a death penalty.

6 Some sources claim it was the pre-Socratic philosopher Pythagoras who came up with this word. I like to imagine Pythagoras thinking about loving wisdom after forbidding his followers from eating beans, and refusing to believe in irrational numbers. A good reminder that wisdom and folly can be neighbours!

7 Thank you Simon Mungall for your humour. IYKYK

8 This is the opening sentence of Rousseau's *The Social Contract.*

9 A version of this conversation actually took place between these philosophers. An account of it can be found in Dietz (1999).

10 This is a paraphrasing of Marx's 1875 *Critique of the Gotha Programme.*

11 This can be translated as Mother Earth.

What Is Political Philosophy? (Or Why You Should Read This Book)

1 The more you think about this … the more you might realise that all ideas and practices are political. What you do, what you think, affects others, affects how we live, affects who we are. In a way, therefore, political philosophy is interested in all aspects of our human experience.

What Do You Want?

1 I imagine someone giving me a bowl of chocolates 'Most of these are safe, just a one might be poisonous'. Um, no thanks. But in reality, life is a bit like this. Every time we eat, or do anything, there is a tiny possibility we get hurt, seriously hurt. But surely, we can't let that worry leads us to do nothing or, even worse, to never have chocolates!

2 This assumes you live in a society where money is used. If you lived by yourself in the jungle, you would not need money. But you will still need the ability to access food and have shelter. You would need health. And as you got older you would probably need support to access food. Also, if you live on your own, have no option to be with someone else, you are not really 'free' to choose to be alone. You have no choice.

3 A similar case went to court in London. Neighbours complained when a townhouse was painted white with red stripes – who does not like candy canes! (Press Association 2017).

4 Conquest's *The Great Terror* is an interesting source here.

5 An interesting source here is Lasch's *The Culture of Narcissism.*

6 Communism is another utopia: an ideal world where everyone owns all things together and everyone works to help others while receiving whatever they need. People are free to do what they want, assuming they will do what is best for all. Of course, the USSR never achieved communism. Instead, the USSR had a large, oppressive government that failed to provide for its population – millions starved and suffered – while also repressing individuality to maintain conformity.

Who Makes You, You?

1 In Hobbes' retelling of this story, he imagines that all the planks that are replaced are collected and used to build a new boat. Or … is this the old boat?

2 An even more severe example – which is mostly just theoretical at the moment – is a head transplant. Not only is this an incredibly complicated procedure but it brings up big questions about where our thoughts and consciousness reside. If we could move your head, your brain, your spinal cord, to a new body, is that the core of you still being you?

3 Nations can be understood as groups of people who feel a shared sense of identity, history, language. This is not the same as a country, which is a geographic place that is considered sovereign. A state is the government that rules a country. Sometimes these three concepts overlap – you have a country with one nation and one state – but that is rare. Usually there are multiple nations in one country.

Why Do We Go to War?

1 There is some interesting science here on the minimum number of humans needed to recreate a human population without the genetic problems of inbreeding – you can research this. I am side-stepping this problem in the chapter.

2 Of course, there was no space travel when Hobbes was alive. But there were boats. The Spanish Armada attacked England when Hobbes was born, and Hobbes said this traumatic event shaped what he thought of human nature and society. He said he was born afraid; afraid of what humans could do to each other as they thought only of their own interests. Hobbes built his philosophy imagining a scenario where there were no rules and human nature was allowed to roam free. He called this the 'state of nature'.

3 This links back to our discussion of freedom in Chapter Five.

4 Carol Gilligan, Joan Tronto, and Nel Noddings are philosophers who work on what is known as care ethics, looking how human's ethics are led by caring for others, rather than just by competition and self-interest.

5 Cato is a pseudonym of *nom de plume* for the author of the essays that argued against Madison, Jay, and Hamilton, who wrote the essays now known as the *Federalist Papers* under the pseudonym *Publius*. Cato's identity is not certain, but it is taught to be George Clinton.

6 If you want to read more on this debate you can read *Federalist Papers* 10 and 2, and *Cato* No. 3.

7 There is some interesting research on the links between population size and violence being done by looking at ants – how large does a colony need to be before they decide to wage warfare rather than using other tactics. Moffett's 'When It Comes to Waging War' is an interesting article on it.

Who Should Rule?

1 Now, my mostly well-behaved cocker spaniel is raising an eyebrow at this phrase and its assumptions about animals. He notes that animals do have rules, they don't just randomly attack each other. But Hobbes was writing in the seventeenth century and thus had limited knowledge of animal science. And, of course, humans are animals too.

2 This is why Thomas Hobbes, John Locke, and Jean Jacques Rousseau are known as social contract theorists – they wrote about this contract between society and the government.

3 This assumes, of course, that parents are indeed keeping kids safe. It also assumes that it is the job of the state to take care of us like children. Many have contested this idea (the nanny state), noting that this view gives too much power to the state and infantilises the people.

4 Ancient Athens had a partial direct democracy. A direct democracy is one where everyone (who is able and willing to vote) votes on every law. Usually whatever the majority votes for wins. In a representative democracy people vote to elect representatives who will act on their behalf in government. Athens did not let everyone vote, however, which is why it is not a full direct democracy.

5 We are still far from equality, however. Women and minorities hold very few leadership roles.

6 In the case of the USA, separation of powers, representative democracy, a bicameral legislative, and an electoral college were put in place as tools to prevent democracy from following bad but popular ideas. You can consider whether it has worked.

7 With thanks to Stuart Lloyd for introducing me to this example.

8 This is why verifying our sources is increasingly important. Find multiple, different sources, read opposing perspectives, analyse arguments critically.

9 Sadly, even more stinky than broccoli, lots of conspiracy theories have gained followers in recent years, leading people to make poor choices when deciding who to vote for. There are conspiracies that say the Earth is flat, that reptiles rule the world, that presidents are zombies ...

10 In this context a tyrant is a ruler who has all the power and uses this power for their own interests, rather than the interests of the people.

11 Historically education has been used as a barrier to political participation. In the USA during the Jim Crow era unfair tests, and unfairly marked tests, were used to prevent African Americans from voting.

12 Some argue that this is already the case in democracy: those with money can organise campaigns, give donations to politicians to influence what they do, and buy media space to get their ideas out. Those without money might even struggle to take time off work to get to vote.

13 This topic will be taken up in Chapter Twelve.

14 Think of the logistics for a second. How do you organise several million people to vote? How do you make sure all votes are safe and not tampered with? What about if some of your citizens live in other countries – will you let them vote? What if they are on the space station – can they still vote? What if they are sick on election day – do they just miss out? Will you make voting mandatory? Will you fine those who do not vote?

Who Owns What?

1 This is a paraphrase of Rousseau's text 'The first man who, having enclosed a piece of ground, bethought himself of saying This is mine, and found people simple enough to believe him, was the real founder of civil society. From how many crimes, wars, and murders, from how many horrors and misfortunes might not any one have saved mankind, by pulling up the stakes, or filling up the ditch, and crying to his fellows: Beware of listening to this impostor; you are undone if you once forget that the fruits of the earth belong to us all, and the earth itself to nobody.' (Rousseau 1913[1755].)

2 The idea that I own something because I have put work into it can be found in Locke's labor theory of value. As Locke states 'Whatsoever, then, he removes out of the state that Nature hath provided and left it in, he hath mixed his labour with it, and joined to it something that is his own, and thereby makes it his property.' (Locke, 1988[1689] Chapter V, Section 27.)

3 When Europeans arrived to what would become known as the Americas, there had already been many centuries of fighting over who owned the land. The Incas, for

instance, were an expanding empire who took over the land of many other indigenous people and made it part of the Inca Empire or Tahuantinsuyo. Similarly in North America the Aztecs took over land through conquest and alliances.

4 Sadly, slavery is not just an evil of the past. There are millions of people around the world currently being held as slaves. The world community needs to work together to find and free these victims.

5 Please note that Marx's perspective was centred on Europe.

6 Ideal is an important word. A utopia is an ideal. Democracy is an ideal. These are ideas that are in theory perfect, but which we might not be able to reach now … or maybe ever. Imagine an ideal day – where everything is just perfect, from a rainbow in the sky, to sun for a picnic in the park during lunch time, to lunch being magically delivered by dancing unicorns, and gentle drifting snow while you read a book or play video games inside your house. Ideals are wonderful to think about, but should they be goals?

7 This is a quote from Marx's Critique of the Gotha Program 1970 (1871).

8 Marxism is in no small part controversial because Marx claimed that religion was used to keep people oppressed. Countries that sought communism repressed all religious faiths.

9 This refers to income taxes. There are other types of taxes. To name just a few: there are property taxes – for example based on what house you own; consumption taxes – for example the government could choose to tax those who drink alcohol arguing that alcohol is not a need, and it is actually not that good for you, so a tax in alcohol is a win-win, they discourage people from drinking and they get money. There are also inheritance taxes. These are taxes you pay on what your ancestors leave you – the idea being to avoid wealth from accumulating in only a few families.

10 I am referring here to government workers who are managing the whole process as well as elected officials who get a salary from the government.

11 This is poor logic as it assumes fires are only caused by personal negligence. Fires can be accidental. They can be unexpected. The most responsible and careful persons can face terrible fires.

12 Sociologist Thorstein Veblen notes that humans don't always buy things at the most reasonable price. People might choose to buy expensive goods – such as branded shoes or purses – not because they are of better quality but to show off their ability to buy this and to gain prestige by doing this. This is called *conspicuous consumption*. People who want to show off their shopping power might opt for a million-dollar flowers. I suggest you use your money in a more sensible way.

Should Humans Be Like Geese?

1 Scotland, for example, boast of the unicorn as its national animal. How cool is that?

2 See Rosales 2007.

3 You can read an apology from the State of California for some of these events here: www.leginfo.ca.gov/pub/05-06/bill/sen/sb_0651-0700/sb_670_bill_20051007_chaptered.html

4 The Universal Declaration of Human Rights was written in part as a response to what state-less people experienced during WWII. The idea is to create a set of rights

protecting all humans regardless of what state they are in. Of course, the question of who would enforce these rights remains problematic.

Should Nature Have Rights?

1 Your gut flora is affected by a variety of things – from what you were fed as an infant, to what your house is cleaned with, to what food you consume. Fermented food, for example, is filled with 'good' bacteria that adds to your gut flora's diversity and health. For those whose gut biome has become deeply unhealthy, doctors might use faecal microbiota transplants, or putting in poo from a healthy donor via a colonoscopy into the guts of the unhealthy person. Yes, a poo transplant. This is how important your gut biome is.
2 See Johnson 2020.
3 This adds a new dimension to our discussion of identity in the first part of this book.
4 Here we could further argue that if these animals were not used, if humans took their place and were paid for their work, it would be poorer humans who might be tempted to sign up for experiments. Thus, it is interesting to consider whether animals are saving the most vulnerable humans from pain.

Is Having Pets Immoral?

1 This is a paraphrase of Bentham's famous phrase, discussed below in the text (Bentham 1907).
2 Descartes 1998 [1637].
3 Bentham 948/1789.
4 See Gigliotti 2022, Birch et al 2021, Andress et al 2024.
5 Andrews et al 2024 – see nydeclaration.com
6 The idea of the social contract has been discussed in the second section of this book.
7 We could note here that feeding cattle to become food (steaks) also requires the use of a great amount of land, and has huge environmental costs. Eating plants is the environmentally sensible thing to do, even if we do not consider other ethical concerns.
8 There is a famous philosophy paper by Thomas Nagel which questions whether humans could ever know what it is like 'to be a bat'. Nagel argues that while we might be able to think about what it would be like to be a bat from a human perspective, we could never know what it is like to be a bat for a bat. Can you imagine what it would be like to be a bat?
9 This links us back to our discussion on identity, which is in the first part of this book.
10 There is space here to discuss how different this relationship has been in different cultures. Different animals are seen as dirty or holy in different cultures and how humans have related to animals is also culturally based.

Would You Like to Become a Cyborg?

1 This has been done with a mouse – mighty mouse is here, why not mighty human? (Case Western Reserve University 2007).
2 The use of race and racism to justice colonisation is expanded on in my other publication (Roitman 2025).

3 We could note here that there are no 'white' people – all people have some colour to their skin. If there was ever a white person, they would be terrifying, very ghost-like, and also unable to survive our sun!

4 Medically intervening to make a person infertile.

5 Ironically, in the word eugenics you might recognise the same root as in utopia – see Chapter Four: A quick note on utopias. Again, it was about seeking the genes of human flourishing, the best genes. Assuming some genes as superior to others.

6 For example, the United States banned Chinese immigrants for 10 years in 1882. On the other hand, Argentina tried to encourage Europeans immigrants to help 'whiten' its population.

7 Alonso and Savulescu 2021.

8 You can look at what Neuralink is working on, for example.

9 Think about how many hours you spend on a smart phone a day – are you and your phone becoming one entity? If you could have your phone integrated into your hand, would you?

10 Interestingly, the idea of all humans being connected to a global intelligence has been around for centuries. Twelfth-century Andalusian philosopher Ibn Rushd, for example, argued for unity of intellect – the idea that humans all share one intellect.

Should We Be Afraid of AI?

1 This also brings up questions of ethics – the ideas computers are using to create 'new' material belong to human creators. Are these creators being acknowledged and paid?

2 Michelle 2024.

3 A robot police.

4 New York, Singapore, and Dubai are three examples of cities looking at this technology.

5 The Innocence Project has done some research in this area.

6 You could look up the 'hungry judge effect' which found that judges were more lenient after having a meal and harsher before lunch – when they were hungrier and grumpier.

7 If you are interested in the ethics of AI, you will enjoy Casey Fiesler's social media content

8 Because AI advances so quickly, there is likely to be some change between when I am writing this and the time you are read this.

9 Let's take a moment to note how cool this name is! Superheroes!

10 This is an ironic link to Frantz Fanon's book *Black Skins White Masks.*

11 Hofmann et al 2024.

12 We cannot underestimate the power of the human mind to seek and find companionship. In a bizarre case a man argued that an AI chat robot encouraged him to try and kill the Queen of England when he broke into Windsor Castle.

How Do You Say Knowledge?

1 I say 'used' rather than spoken because there are non-spoken languages, including sign languages. This chapter focuses mostly on spoken and written languages. Sign

languages also fit into the discussion, however, given their grammar and construction, and how they have been used/ignored by those in power.

2 There is some interesting research about how different people's brains process language that is relevant here. Some people do not create mental 'images' of what they read/hear/think about. They think about the concept, but they do not 'see' it. This is called *aphantasia*. Going back to Molyneux's problem, a person with aphantasia might face the problem differently than someone who is able to create mental images.

3 If you enjoy linguistics as much as me, the work of Adam Aleksic is worth exploring.

4 A couple of fascinating papers on this are Bergen and Ting 2012 and Tversky et al 1991.

5 Famously, Pepsi's slogan 'Come alive with the Pepsi generation' was wrongly translated into Chinese as 'Pepsi brings your ancestors back from the grave'. In 2009 HSBC Bank's campaign was mistranslated from 'Assume Nothing' to 'Do Nothing'. Mistranslations in times of war can be dangerous rather than humorous, highlighting the need to rely on humans rather than computers for translation. In WWII the USA relied on Navajo speakers as a way to send messages which enemies could not decipher, and which had the added benefit of immediate human understanding.

6 Neuroscience is also expanding our understanding of how our brain processes language and thoughts – and how different areas of our brain may use language differently. Some research for example, seems to show that our right brain hemisphere is concerned with intent in reaching moral decisions. There is much to learn about how we truly reason. For more on this you can read Gazzaniga 2005 and Steckler et al 2017.

Should the Government Pay for Opera?

1 Another great thinker who mentions the inspiration and change that can come from awe is China's Su Tung-po:

Peer at things up close and you may learn their true form,
but guessed at from afar, they seem like something else.
Vastness such as this is beyond comprehension –
All I can do is sight in endless wonder. (Cited in Weiner 2016.)

2 Because of space constraints I am not drawing enough of a difference between beauty and the sublime. For philosophers the sublime was not the same as beauty. It was much greater. For Burke it could even be terrifying. Like standing at night on a mountain peak seeing the Milky Way and realising the enormity of the universe. The sublime transforms us by its power. Beauty is also transformative but it is only a possible, limited path, to the truly sublime. We should also note that not all art is beautiful – even while it might be sublime.

Does the Past Affect the Future?

1 The italicised section is a quote from Edward Said, *Orientalism*, 1978.

2 This allegory was explained in the chapter on education.

3 That is with a questioning lens – asking questions about why, and how, and whether this is the right way.
4 For an overview of the use of non-white bodies in US medical research you can read Nuriddin, A., Mooney, G., & White, A. I. R. (2020).
5 The terms Global North and Global South are used to differentiate wealthier countries of the geographic north who participated and benefit from colonisation, from those in the global south who are suffering with greater poverty. This is not an entirely geographic label as Australia and New Zealand are in the Global North.
6 Most universities now require research to be approved by an ethics committee which should review the research to ensure it causes no harm and is only undertaken with the informed consent of those participating. However, one might still question to what extent people who speak a different language and who have limited understanding of 'academic language' can understand what research entails and leads to.
7 It is estimated, for instance, that Spain took out 40,000 tonnes of silver from Potosi in Bolivia. This made Spain incredibly wealthy. Meanwhile Bolivia is one of the poorest countries in Latin America.
8 Archaeologist Khaled as-Asaad was killed when trying to guard Syrian historical artifacts from ISIS. After the fall Saddam Hussein's regime in 2003, thousands of historical artifacts were looted and sold in the black market.
9 The book has also tried to discuss decolonisation in other chapters as relevant to the topic. For example, we discussed language imperialism, ownership and reparation, and immigration and justice.

How Can We Build a Just World?

1 This is actually a poor solution as we would be left with a lot of decomposing bodies which release CO_2. Perhaps we could send half of humanity into space? But then that requires a LOT of energy …
2 You might note a connection between this discussion and our discussion in Chapter Five on the trade-off between freedom and safety.
3 I should note here that Anscombe did note some actions were always unjustifiable – such as killing the innocent. However, her reasoning was different from Kant's.
4 That is, it might decide something should never or always be done based on what religious texts/guides state. On the other hand, religion might also have a consequential approach to justice – European religious leaders, for example, argued that killing indigenous people in the Americas was just as this led them to heaven rather than hell.
5 This links back to our discussion of decolonisation in Chapter Eighteen.

Conclusion

1 Please note these are fictitious, not real quotes.

Printed in the United States
by Baker & Taylor Publisher Services